AIR FRYER COOKBOOK FOR BEGINNERS

1200 Days of Easy & Delicious Recipes, in Alphabetic Order, to Learn How to Fry, Grill & Bake. Discover all the Secrets to Become an Effortless Professional

Stacy Haves

TABLE OF CONTENTS

INTRODUCTION

WHAT IS THE AIR FRYER?

Air Fryer is a popular and wholesome appliance to adapt to your kitchen counter. It lets you cook something perfectly and excellently, thanks to its hot air circulation system. The top of the unit contains a heating mechanism and a fan: the hot air flows downwards until it "embraces" the food placed in a special frying basket. Its primary function is to harness heat by convection, and that is, to trap hot air by swirling around the food to cook it on the spot.

These tolls use a special technology called rapid air circulation, therefore, all the food is succulent inside and perfectly cooked outside. Using an Air Fryer, you can enjoy fried food without adding extra calories and fat since it cooks food using minimal grease and oil and sometimes even without. It makes food perfectly crispy outside and tender and juicy inside. It allows you to cook, bake, steam and roast pretty much everything you can imagine. This mechanism makes the food crispy, just like fried food.

Furthermore, its small size makes cooking much faster. But what is the air fryer excellent for? Basically, it reduces calories by drastically reducing (or zeroing) oil consumption. The size also makes it easy to clean after use, and most air fryers have removable parts that fit in the dishwasher.

WHAT INGREDIENTS TO COOK IN THE AIR FRYER

The air fryer works like a small oven, so it is very suitable for all cooking that requires dry heat. Basically, you can prepare roasted or breaded meat or fish dishes in it very well, but it is not ideal for steaming or preparing boiled dishes. It is perfect for frozen or pre-fried preparations, like those found in the supermarket. But it is even better to prepare lighter versions of fancy food that we would normally fry, but with little fat!

The air fryer also works very well with vegetables, especially those for grilling, like zucchini, eggplant, broccoli, cauliflower, and squash. And it is ideal for making potatoes, which with a few tips will come out perfect! As it works like a small oven, you can even bake bread there, or use it for puff pastries. And even cakes! Muffins with shortcrust batter, just follow the directions. Finally, this is an excellent quick way to warm up leftover food, especially if it needs to come back crispy!

DOES THE AIR FRYER NEED OIL?

Although some recipes do not need it, most require it even in significantly smaller quantities than in traditional frying. Almost always 1-2 teaspoons of oil are enough, whereas, for breaded foods, it is better to "abound" with 1-2 tablespoons. Usually, simply brush it directly onto the food, while you can proceed by combining the oil with the breadcrumbs.

RULES TO NEVER FORGET!

1. **PREHEAT YOUR AIR FRYER FIRST:** this is a crucial step and is used to ensure even cooking, so don't skip it!

2. **TAKE SAFETY PRECAUTIONS:** Only hold the air fryer basket by the handle. If you touch any other part of the basket, you will get burned. Some air fryers come with a pan that fits the basket (or the pans can be purchased separately). Make sure you use oven mitts or a potholder to remove the pan. Also, make sure you put the air fryer on a flat, heat resistant surface with several inches of space around all parts of the fryer. The air fryer is a mini-oven and will get super-hot!

3. **SPRAY YOUR FOOD TRAY/BASKET WITH OIL BEFORE COOKING:** regardless of the food you want to prepare, grease the basket of the air fryer with a little oil so that the food does not stick during cooking. Very little is really needed, and a clever trick is to use a spray bottle of oil, which allows you to create a thin, even film! Oil is also necessary to leave food moist; if you don't use it, dry, tough dishes will come out.

4. **ADD A LITTLE OIL TO YOUR VEGGIES:** You don't need a lot, but a little bit of oil will help your veggies get brown and crispy. You can do this by spraying your veggies with some oil. Frozen veggies turn out better than fresh ones.

5. **ADD SOME WATER TO THE BASKET FOR MEAT:** This is an awesome trip! If you add a little bit of water to the basket underneath the cooking tray, it will help prevent excess smoking as your meat is cooking. The grease will drip into the water. It will also make clean-up much easier!

6. **ALWAYS USE THE APPROPRIATE GRILL:** it is located directly in the basket! It is this, in fact, that allows the hot air to circulate around the food and cook the food perfectly. The air fryer, in fact, cooks by convection, that is, it creates a vortex of hot air, somewhat like a very powerful small, ventilated oven.

7. **DON'T FILL THE BASKET TOO FULL:** once you are ready to cook, do not overfill the basket even when foods seem to be going comfortably in it, otherwise, the cooking will be uneven! Consider, based on the model you own, how many people you can cook for and how much weight in ingredients.

8. **STIR THE FOOD OCCASIONALLY:** to have perfect "frying," stir the food occasionally. It serves to get the heat well everywhere. So, take the basket out at least a couple of times, shake it a bit, and put it back in. Don't worry! When you take the basket out, the machine will automatically stop, to start cooking again once it is inserted again.

9. **CLEAN YOUR AIR FRYER REGULARLY:** It's always tempting to leave an appliance uncleaned. However, if you don't clean your air fryer regularly, it might start smoking, and it will get more and more difficult to clean, which could lead to damage, wear, and tear. Always allow the appliance to cool completely before cleaning. Clean the pan and basket with hot water, a little dish soap, and a non-abrasive sponge. Clean other parts of the inside with just hot water and a sponge. You may need to lean the heater element with a stiff cleaning brush to remove food residue.

WHY USE AIR FRYER?

Many people have a love-hate relationship with fried foods. While they wish they could erase the calories they receive from it, they also love the taste and crunch that comes with it. That is where the air fryer comes in. The air fryer stands out from its competitors' appliances because it offers a low-fat version of normally unhealthy foods such as fried chicken, french fries, and onion rings.

As some healthy foods tend to have a knock-off taste from the real deal, air fryers produce a delicious taste and feel in your mouth. The air fryer can be used in many ways to help make your. daily life more manageable. Whether you want to fry, bake, grill, or roast ingredients, the air fryer can do it all. It can cook without oil, prepare multiple dishes at once, and its parts can be easily removed for cleaning.

BENEFITS OF AIR FRYERS

1. **AIR FRYING IS HEALTHY:** compared directly to deep fat frying, food cooked in an air fryer is much more healthy. You will use little to no oil in preparing your food.
2. **AIR FRYING IS QUICK:** the convection fan in your air fryer moves super-heated air around your food very quickly. This means cooking can be as much as 20-30% quicker than using a regular oven.
3. **AIR FRYING CAN SAVE ENERGY:** when you switch your regular oven on, you have to heat a huge cavernous cooking space. If you're like me, often, you will only be preparing a small amount of food too – resulting in a huge waste of energy. With their relatively small internal cooking space, air fryers heat up much more quickly, have less space to maintain heat, plus cool down quicker. The result is usually less energy used.
4. **AIR FRYING CAN HELP YOUR AC IN THE SUMMER:** I hate turning my oven on in the Summer months. That huge oven area has to be heated, it has to be kept at temperature, and it has to cool when you switch it off; that heat enters your home, which your AC, in turn, has to work hard to offset. If you live somewhere where you rely on your AC to work at its very best, you don't want to pump all that extra heat into your home.
5. **GREAT FOR UNIQUELY SMALL KITCHEN SPACE:** for those who might not have a full kitchen's luxury, an air fryer can represent a very flexible and functional way to cook, heat, and reheat.

WHAT CAN BE "FRIED" IN THE AIR FRYER?

One of the marvels of the Air Fryer lies in its ability to do anything, from significant appetizers to everyday dishes.

Here are some tips for air frying proteins, veggies, and frozen foods. Acquaint yourself with the basics, and don't forget to follow the Air Fryer chart with all of the temperatures and cook times so you can consult it anytime. Remember that cook times vary based on the size and quantity of foods placed in the air fryer. You can also open the air fryer during the cooking to check ingredients. Unlike an oven, that will have a dramatic temperature drop, the fryer heats so fast it won't hinder the cooking process.

MEAT AND POULTRY

You can cook all kinds of meat in an air fryer and get delicious results. Just keep in mind that meat cooking times depend on the thickness and desired level of doneness. This means that it's always best to use a thermometer to check your meat's temperature at its thickest. You can get meat temperature zuide here, and if you don't have a cooking thermometer yet, this one is budget-friendly and super useful for cooking and grilling.

SEAFOOD

To get crispy, flakey fish, make sure you don't overcrowd your fryer basket. If there isn't enough space for air to circulate between every seafood piece, they may come out more like they were steamed. It's also a good idea to shake the basket every couple of minutes when cooking smaller items like shrimp and calamari, so you get a nice even cook from every angle.

VEGETABLES

You can cook any veggies in the Air Fryer that will result in a texture that is most similar to roasting yet is crispier on the outside. After you prep your vegetables, we recommend sprinkling just a little oil on them before air frying. Not only will this make them positively yummy, but recent studies also show that a little bit of fat must be present for your body to absorb all of those good carotenoids. Unsurprisingly, soft vegetables will cook quickly, while rough and tough roots will take a little longer.

PREPARED FROZEN FOODS

Whenever cooking takes too much out of you after a long day at work, your trusty air fryer is ready to send your microwave packing with its ability to heat premade frozen foods to perfection. Breaded items like chicken tenders and onion rings will get a satisfyingly airy crunch, while mini pizzas and potstickers will end up with just the right amount of crispness. For any food you need to flip halfway through, grab a pair of silicone-tipped tongs, so you don't scratch the bottom of your fryer.

EXTRA FUN

We only scraped the surface of what you can do with a fryer, so let's cover a little more favorite fun for you.

If you want to make an ordinary bowl of ice cream special, whip up a quick batch of air-fried bananas! And if you want to add crispy tofu to any Meatless Monday dinner, the air fryer is a great way to go – just make sure to press extra water out of it (place a heavy pan on top for a few minutes) before you stick it in the fryer.

AIR FRYER COOKING CHART

BEEF	Temperature (°F)	Time (minutes)
Burger (4 oz.)	370°F	16 to 20
Beef Eye Round Roast (4 lbs.)	390°F	45 to 55
Filet Mignon (8 oz.)	400°F	18
Flank Steak (1.5 lbs.)	400°F	12
London Broil (2 lbs)	400°f	20 to 28
Meatballs (1-inch)	380°F	7
Meatballs (3-inch)	380°F	10
Ribeye, bone-in (1-inch. 12 oz.)	400°F	10 to 15
Sirloin steaks (1-inch, 12 oz.)	400°F	9 to 14

PORK AND LAMB	Temperature (°F)	Time (minutes)
Bacon (regular)	400°F	5 to 7
Bacon (thick cut)	400°F	6 to 10
Lamb Loin Chops (1-inch thick)	400°F	8 to 12
Loin (2 lbs)	360°F	55
Pork Chops, bone in (1-inch, 6.5 oz.)	400°F	12
Rack of Lamb (1.5-2 lbs.)	380°F	22
Sausages	380°F	15
Tenderloin (1 lb.)	370°F	15

CHICKEN	Temperature (°F)	Time (minutes)
Breasts, bone in (1.25 lbs)	370°F	25

Breasts, boneless (4 oz.)	380°F	12
Drumsticks (2.5 lbs.)	370°F	20
Game Hen (halved-2 lbs.)	390°F	20
Legs, bone in (1.75 lbs.)	380°F	30
Tenders	360°F	8-10
Thighs, bone in (2 lbs.)	380°F	22
Thighs, boneless (1.5 lbs.)	380°F	18 to 20
Whole Chicken (6.5 lbs.)	360°F	65
Wings (2 lbs.)	400°F	12

FISH AND SEAFOOD	Temperature (°F)	Time (minutes)
Calamari (8 oz.9	400°F	4
Fish Fillet (1-inch, 8 oz.)	400°F	10
Salmon Fillet (6 oz.)	380°F	12
Scallops	400°F	5 to 7
Shrimps	400°F	5
Swordfifh Steak	400°F	10
Tuna Steak	400°F	7 to 10

VEGETABLES	Temp	Time (minutes)
Asparagus (sliced 1-inch)	400°F	5
Beets (whole)	400°F	40
Broccoli (florets)	400°F	6
Brussels Sprouts (halved)	380°F	15
Carrots (sliced ½-inch)	380°F	15

Cauliflower (florets)	400°F	12
Corn on the Cob	390°F	6
Eggplant (1 ½-inch cubes)	370°F	15
Fennel (quartered)	370°F	15
Green Beans	400°F	5
Kale Leaves	250°F	12
Mushrooms (sliced ¼-inch)	400°F	5
Onions (pearl)	400°F	10
Parsnips (1/2-inch chunks)	380°F	15
Peppers (1-inch chunks)	400°F	15
Potatoes (1-inch chunks)	400°F	15
Potatoes (small baby, 1.5 lbs.)	400°F	15
Potatoes (baked whole)	400°F	40
Squash (1/2-inch chunks)	400°F	12
Sweet Potatoes (baked)	380°F	30 to 35
Tomatoes (cherry)	400°F	4
Tomatoes (halved)	350°F	10
Zucchini (1/2-inch sticks)	400°F	12

FROZEN FOODS	Temperature (°F)	Time (minutes)
Breaded Shrimps	400°F	9
Chicken Nuggets (12 oz.9	400°F	10
Fish Fillets (1/2-inch 10 oz.)	400°F	14
Fish Sticks (10 oz.)	400°F	10
Mozzarella Sticks (11 oz.)	400°F	8

Onion rings (12 oz.)	400°F	8
Pot Stickers (10 oz.)	400°F	8
Thick French Fries (17 oz.)	400°F	18
Thin French Fries (20 oz.)	400°F	14

BREAKFAST

1. Air Fryer Sandwich

Preparation time: 10 minutes **Cooking time:** 6 minutes **Servings:** 2

Ingredients:

- 2 English muffins, halved
- 2 eggs
- 2 bacon strips
- Salt and black pepper

Directions:

1. Crack eggs in your Air Fryer, add bacon on top, cover and cook at 392°F for 6 minutes.
2. Heat up your English muffin halves in your microwave for a few seconds, divide eggs into 2 halves, add bacon on top, season with salt and pepper, cover with the other 2 English muffins and serve.
3. Enjoy!

Nutrition: calories 261, fat 5, fiber 8, carbs 12, protein 4

2. Blackberry French Toast

Preparation time: 10 minutes **Cooking time:** 20 minutes **Servings:** 6

Ingredients:

- 1 cup blackberry jam, warm
- 12 ounces bread loaf, cubed

- 8 ounces cream cheese, cubed
- 4 eggs
- 1 teaspoon cinnamon powder
- 2 cups half and half
- ½ cup brown sugar
- 1 teaspoon vanilla extract
- Cooking spray

Directions:

1. Grease your Air Fryer with cooking spray and heat it up to 300°F.
2. Add blueberry jam on the bottom, layer half of the bread cubes, then add cream cheese and top with the rest of the bread.
3. In a bowl, mix eggs with half-and-half, cinnamon, sugar and vanilla, whisk well and add over bread mix.
4. Cook for 20 minutes and divide among plates. Enjoy!

Nutrition: calories 261, fat 5, fiber 8, carbs 12, protein 4

3. Breakfast Doughnuts

Preparation time: 10 minutes **Cooking time:** 18 minutes **Servings:** 6

Ingredients:

- 4 tablespoons butter, soft
- 1 and ½ teaspoon baking powder
- 2 and ¼ cups white flour
- ½ cup sugar
- 1/3 cup caster sugar
- 1 teaspoon cinnamon powder
- 2 egg yolks
- ½ cup sour cream

Directions:

1. In a bowl, mix 2 tablespoons of butter with simple sugar and egg yolks and whisk well.
2. Add half of the sour cream and stir.

3. In another bowl, mix flour with baking powder, stir and also add to the egg mix.
4. Stir well until you obtain a dough, transfer it to a floured working surface, roll it out and cut big circles with smaller ones in the middle.
5. Brush doughnuts with the rest of the butter, heat up your Air Fryer at 360°F, place doughnuts inside and cook them for 8 minutes. In a bowl, mix cinnamon with caster sugar and stir.
6. Arrange doughnuts on plates and dip them in cinnamon and sugar before serving.
7. Enjoy!

Nutrition: calories 182, fat 3, fiber 7, carbs 8, protein 3

4. Breakfast Potatoes

Preparation time: 10 minutes **Cooking time:** 35 minutes **Servings:** 4

Ingredients:

- 2 tablespoons olive oil
- 3 potatoes, cubed
- 1 yellow onion, chopped
- 1 red bell pepper, chopped
- Salt and black pepper to the taste
- 1 teaspoon garlic powder
- 1 teaspoon sweet paprika
- 1 teaspoon onion powder

Directions:

1. Grease your Air Fryer's basket with olive oil, add potatoes, toss and season with salt and pepper.
2. Add onion, bell pepper, garlic powder, paprika and onion powder, toss well, cover and cook at 370°F for 30 minutes. Divide potatoes mix on plates and serve for breakfast. Enjoy!

Nutrition: calories 214, fat 6, fiber 8, carbs 15, protein

5. Breakfast Veggie Mix

Preparation time: 10 minutes **Cooking time:** 25 minutes **Servings:** 6

Ingredients:

- 1 yellow onion, sliced
- 1 red bell pepper, chopped
- 1 gold potato, chopped
- 2 tablespoons olive oil
- 8 ounces brie, trimmed and cubed
- 12 ounces sourdough bread, cubed
- 4 ounces Parmesan, grated
- 8 eggs
- 2 tablespoons mustard
- 3 cups milk
- Salt and black pepper to the taste

Directions:

1. Heat up your Air Fryer at 350°F, add oil, onion, potato and bell pepper and cook for 5 minutes.
2. In a bowl, mix eggs with milk, salt, pepper and mustard and whisk well.
3. Add bread and brie to your Air Fryer, add half of the eggs mix and add half of the Parmesan.
4. Add the rest of the bread and Parmesan, toss just a little, and cook for 20 minutes.
5. Divide among plates. Enjoy!

Nutrition: calories 231, fat 5, fiber 10, carbs 20, protein 12

6. Buttermilk Breakfast Biscuits

Preparation time: 10 minutes **Cooking time:** 8 minutes **Servings:** 4

Ingredients:

- 1 and ¼ cup white flour
- ½ cup self-rising flour
- ¼ teaspoon baking soda
- ½ teaspoon baking powder
- 1 teaspoon sugar

- 4 tablespoons butter, cold and cubed+ 1 tablespoon melted butter
- ¾ cup buttermilk
- Maple syrup for serving

Directions:

1. In a bowl, mix white flour with self-rising flour, baking soda, baking powder and sugar and stir.
2. Add cold butter and stir using your hands.
3. Add buttermilk, stir until you obtain a dough and transfer to a floured working surface.
4. Roll your dough and cut 10 pieces using a round cutter.
5. Arrange biscuits in your Air Fryer's cake pan, brush them with melted butter and cook at 400°F for 8 minutes.
6. Serve them for breakfast with some maple syrup on top. Enjoy!

Nutrition: calor 192, fat 6, fiber 9, carbs 12, protein 3

7. Creamy Breakfast Tofu

Preparation time: 15 minutes **Cooking time:** 20 minutes **Servings:** 4

Ingredients:

- 1 block firm tofu, pressed and cubed
- 1 teaspoon rice vinegar
- 2 tablespoons soy sauce
- 2 teaspoons sesame oil
- 1 tablespoon potato starch
- 1 cup Greek yogurt

Directions:

1. In a bowl, mix tofu cubes with vinegar, soy sauce and oil, toss, and leave aside for 15 minutes.
2. Dip tofu cubes in potato starch, toss, transfer to your Air Fryer, heat up to 370°F and cook for 20 minutes, shaking halfway.
3. Divide into bowls and serve for breakfast with some Greek yogurt on the side. Enjoy!

Nutrition: calori 110, fat 4, fiber 5, carbs 8, protein 4

8. Creamy Eggs

Preparation time: 10 minutes **Cooking time:** 12 minutes **Servings:** 4

Ingredients:

- 2 teaspoons butter, soft
- 2 ham slices
- 4 eggs
- 2 tablespoons heavy cream
- Salt and black pepper to the taste
- 3 tablespoons parmesan, grated
- 2 teaspoons chives, chopped
- A pinch of smoked paprika

Directions:

1. In a bowl, mix tofu cubes with vinegar, soy sauce and oil, toss, and leave aside for 15 minutes.
2. Dip tofu cubes in potato starch, toss, transfer to your Air Fryer, heat up to 370°F and cook for 20 minutes, shaking halfway.
3. Divide into bowls and serve for breakfast with some Greek yogurt on the side. Enjoy! Grease your Air Fryer's pan with the butter, line it with the ham and add it to your Air Fryer's basket.
4. In a bowl, mix 1 egg with heavy cream, salt, and pepper, whisk well and add over ham.
5. Crack the rest of the eggs in the pan, sprinkle Parmesan and cook your mix for 12 minutes at 320°F. Sprinkle paprika and chives all over, divide among plates and serve for breakfast.

Nutrition: calor 263, fat 5, fiber 8, carbs 12, protein 5

9. Creamy Hash Browns

Preparation time: 10 minutes **Cooking time:** 20 minutes **Servings:** 6

Ingredients:

- 2 pounds hash browns

- 1 cup whole milk
- 8 bacon slices, chopped
- 9 ounces cream cheese
- 1 yellow onion, chopped
- 1 cup cheddar cheese, shredded
- 6 green onions, chopped
- Salt and black pepper
- 6 eggs
- Cooking spray

Directions:

1. Heat up your Air Fryer at 350°F and grease it with cooking spray.
2. In a bowl, mix eggs with milk, cream cheese, cheddar cheese, bacon, onion, salt and pepper and whisk well.
3. Add hash browns to your Air Fryer, add eggs mix over them and cook for 20 minutes.
4. Divide among plates and serve. Enjoy!

Nutrition: calori 261, fat 6, fiber 9, carbs 8, protein 12

10. Egg Muffins

Preparation time: 10 minutes **Cooking time:** 15 minutes **Servings:** 4

Ingredients:

- 1 egg
- 2 tablespoons olive oil
- 3 tablespoons milk
- 3.5 ounces white flour
- 1 tablespoon baking powder
- 2 ounces Parmesan, grated
- A splash of Worcestershire sauce

Directions:

1. In a bowl, mix egg with flour, oil, baking powder, milk, Worcestershire, and Parmesan, whisk well and divide into 4 silicone muffin cups.
2. Arrange cups in your Air Fryer's cooking basket, cover and cook at 392°F for 15 minutes. Enjoy!

Nutrition: calori 251, fat 6, fiber 8, carbs 9, protein 3

11. Fast Eggs and Tomatoes

Preparation time: 5 minutes **Cooking time:** 10 minutes **Servings:** 4

Ingredients:

- 4 eggs
- 2 ounces milk
- 2 tablespoons Parmesan, grated
- Salt and black pepper to the taste
- 8 cherry tomatoes, halved
- Cooking spray

Directions:

1. Grease your Air Fryer with cooking spray and heat it up to 200°F.
2. In a bowl, mix eggs with cheese, milk, salt and pepper and whisk.
3. Add this mix to your Air Fryer and cook for 6 minutes.
4. Add tomatoes, cook your scrambled eggs for 3 minutes, divide among plates. Enjoy!

Nutrition: calories 200, fat 4, fiber 7, carbs 12, protein 3

12. Ham Breakfast Pie

Preparation time: 10 minutes. **Cooking time:** 25 minutes **Servings:** 6

Ingredients:

- 16 ounces crescent rolls dough
- 2 eggs, whisked

- 2 cups cheddar cheese, grated
- 1 tablespoon Parmesan, grated
- 2 cups ham, cooked and chopped
- Salt and black pepper
- Cooking spray

Directions:

1. Grease your Air Fryer's pan with cooking spray and press half of the crescent roll's dough on the bottom.
2. In a bowl, mix eggs with cheddar cheese, Parmesan, salt and pepper, whisk well and add over dough.
3. Spread ham, cut the rest of the crescent roll's dough into strips, arrange them over the ham and cook at 300°F for 25 minutes.
4. Slice pie and serve for breakfast. Enjoy!

Nutrition calories 400, fat 27, fiber 7, carbs 22, protein 16

13. Mushroom Oatmeal

Preparation time: 10 minutes **Cooking time:** 20 minutes **Servings:** 4

Ingredients:

- 1 small yellow onion, chopped
- 1 cup steel-cut oats
- 2 garlic cloves, minced
- 2 tablespoons butter
- ½ cup water
- 14 ounces canned chicken stock
- 3 thyme springs, chopped
- 2 tablespoons extra virgin olive oil
- ½ cup Gouda cheese, grated
- 8 ounces mushroom, sliced
- Salt and black pepper to the taste

Directions:

1. Heat up a pan that fits your Air Fryer with the butter over medium heat, add onions and garlic, stir and cook for 4 minutes.

2. Add oats, water, salt, pepper, stock and thyme, stir, introduce in your Air Fryer and cook at 360°F for 16 minutes.
3. Meanwhile, heat up a pan with the olive oil over medium heat, add mushrooms, cook them for 3 minutes, add to oatmeal and cheese, stir, divide into bowls. Enjoy!

Nutrition: calories 284, fat 8, fiber 8, carbs 20, pro 17

14. Sausage, Eggs and Cheese Mix

Preparation time: 10 minutes **Cooking time:** 20 minutes **Servings:** 4

Ingredients:

- 10 ounces sausages, cooked and crumbled
- 1 cup cheddar cheese, shredded
- 1 cup mozzarella cheese, shredded
- 8 eggs, whisked
- 1 cup milk
- Salt and black pepper
- Cooking spray

Directions:

1. In a bowl, mix sausages with cheese, mozzarella, eggs, milk, salt and pepper and whisk well.
2. Heat up your Air Fryer at 380°F, spray cooking oil, add eggs and sausage mixture and cook for 20 minutes.
3. Divide among plates and serve. Enjoy!

Nutrition: calories 320, fat 6, fiber 8, carbs 12, prot 5

15. Scrambled Eggs

Preparation time: 10 minutes **Cooking time:** 10 minutes **Servings:** 2

Ingredients:

- 2 eggs
- 2 tablespoons butter
- Salt and black pepper to the taste
- 1 red bell pepper, chopped
- A pinch of sweet paprika

14

Directions:

1. In a bowl, mix eggs with salt, pepper, paprika and red bell pepper and whisk well.
2. Heat up your Air Fryer at 140°F, add butter and melt it.
3. Add eggs mix, stir and cook for 10 minutes.
4. Divide scrambled eggs on plates. Enjoy!

Nutrition: calor 200, fat 4, fiber 7, carbs 10, protein 3

16. Smoked Air Fried Tofu Breakfast

Preparation time: 10 minutes **Cooking time:** 12 minutes **Servings:** 2

Ingredients:

- 1 tofu block, pressed and cubed
- Salt and black pepper to the taste
- 1 tablespoon smoked paprika
- ¼ cup cornstarch
- Cooking spray

Directions:

1. Grease your Air Fryer's basket with cooking spray and heat the fryer at 370°F.
2. In a bowl, mix tofu with salt, pepper, smoked paprika and cornstarch and toss well.
3. Add tofu to your Air Fryer's basket and cook for 12 minutes shaking the fryer every 4 minutes.
4. Divide into bowls and serve.

5. Enjoy!

Nutrition: calories 172, fat 4, fiber 7, carbs 12, protein 4

17. Smoked Sausage Breakfast Mix

Preparation time: 10 minutes **Cooking time:** 30 minutes **Servings:** 4

Ingredients:

- 1 and ½ pounds smoked sausage, chopped and browned A pinch of salt and black pepper
- 1 and ½ cups grits
- 4 and ½ cups of water
- 16 ounces cheddar cheese, shredded
- 1 cup milk
- ¼ teaspoon garlic powder
- 1 and ½ teaspoons thyme, chopped
- Cooking spray
- 4 eggs, whisked

Directions:

1. Put the water in a pot, bring to a boil over medium heat, add grits, stir, cover, cook for 5 minutes and take off the heat.
2. Add cheese, stir until it melts and mix with milk, thyme, salt, pepper, garlic powder and eggs and whisk really well.
3. Heat up your Air Fryer at 300°F, grease with cooking spray and add browned sausage. Add grits mix, spread and cook for 25 minutes.
4. Divide among plates.

5. Enjoy!

Nutrition: calories 321, fat 6, fiber 7, carbs 17, protein 4

18. Special Corn Flakes Breakfast Casserole

Preparation time: 10 minutes **Cooking time:** 8 minutes **Servings:** 5

Ingredients:

- 1/3 cup milk
- 3 teaspoons sugar
- 2 eggs, whisked
- ¼ teaspoon nutmeg, ground
- ¼ cup blueberries

- 4 tablespoons cream cheese, whipped
- 1 and ½ cups corn flakes, crumbled
- 5 bread slices

Directions:

1. In a bowl, mix eggs with sugar, nutmeg and milk and whisk well.
2. In another bowl, mix cream cheese with blueberries and whisk well.
3. Put corn flakes in a third bowl.
4. Spread blueberry mix on each bread slice, then dip in eggs mix and dredge in corn flakes at the end.
5. Place bread in your Air Fryer's basket, heat up at 400°F, and bake for 8 minutes.
6. Divide among plates. Enjoy!

Nutrition: calories 300, fat 5, fiber 7, carbs 16, protein 4

19. Tasty Hash Browns

Preparation time: 10 minutes **Cooking time:** 15 minutes **Servings:** 6

Ingredients:

- 16 ounces hash browns
- ¼ cup olive oil
- ½ teaspoon paprika
- ½ teaspoon garlic powder
- Salt and black pepper to the taste
- 1 egg, whisked
- 2 tablespoon chives, chopped
- 1 cup cheddar, shredded

Directions:

1. Add oil to your Air Fryer, heat it up at 350°F and add hash browns.
2. Also add paprika, garlic powder, salt, pepper and egg, toss and cook for 15 minutes.
3. Add cheddar and chives, toss, divide among plates and serve. Enjoy!

Nutrition: calor 213, fat 7, fiber 8, carbs 12, protein 4

20. Tofu and Mushrooms

Preparation time: 10 minutes **Cooking time:** 10 minutes **Servings:** 2

Ingredients:

- 1 tofu block, pressed and cut into medium pieces
- 1 cup panko breadcrumbs
- salt and black pepper
- ½ tablespoons flour
- 1 egg
- 1 tablespoon mushrooms, minced

Directions:

1. In a bowl, mix egg with mushrooms, flour, salt and pepper and whisk well.
2. Dip tofu pieces in egg mix, then dredge them in panko breadcrumbs, place them in your Air Fryer and cook at 350°F for 10 minutes. Serve.
3. Enjoy!

Nutrition: calories 142, fat 4, fiber 6, carbs 8, protein 3

21. Tomato and Bacon Breakfast

Preparation time: 10 minutes **Cooking time:** 30 minutes **Servings:** 6

Ingredients:

- 1-pound white bread, cubed
- 1-pound smoked bacon, cooked and chopped
  ¼ cup olive oil
- 1 yellow onion, chopped
- 28 ounces canned tomatoes, chopped
- ½ teaspoon red pepper, crushed
- ½ pound cheddar, shredded
- 2 tablespoons chives, chopped
- ½ pound Monterey jack, shredded
- 2 tablespoons stock
- Salt and black pepper
- 8 eggs, whisked

Directions:

1. Add the oil to your Air Fryer and heat it up at 350°F. Add bread, bacon, onion, tomatoes, red pepper and stock and stir.
2. Add eggs, cheddar and Monterey jack and cook everything for 20 minutes.
3. Divide among plates, sprinkle chives and serve. Enjoy!

Nutrition: calor 231, fat 5, fiber 7, carbs 12, protein 4

22. Walnuts and Pear Oatmeal

Preparation time: 5 minutes **Cooking time:** 12 minutes **Servings:** 4

Ingredients:

- 1 cup water
- 1 tablespoon butter, soft
- ¼ cup brown sugar
- ½ teaspoon cinnamon powder
- 1 cup rolled oats
- ½ cup walnuts, chopped
- 2 cups pear, peeled and chopped
- ½ cup raisins

Directions:

1. In a heat-proof dish that fits your Air Fryer, mix milk with sugar, butter, oats, cinnamon, raisins, pears and walnuts, stir, introduce to your fryer and cook at 360°F for 12 minutes.
2. Divide into bowls and serve. Enjoy!

Nutrition: calories 230, fat 6, fiber 11, carbs 20, protein 5

23. Rice, Almonds, and Raisins Pudding

Preparation time: 5 minutes **Cooking time:** 8 minutes

Servings: 4

Ingredients:

- 1 cup brown rice

- ½ cup coconut chips
- 1 cup milk
- 2 cups water
- ½ cup maple syrup
- ¼ cup raisins
- ¼ cup almonds
- A pinch of cinnamon powder

Directions:

1. Put the rice in a pan that fits your Air Fryer, add the water, heat up on the stove over medium- high heat, cook until the rice is soft and drain.
2. Add milk, coconut chips, almonds, raisins, cinnamon, and maple syrup, stir well, introduce in Air Fryer and cook at 360° F for 8 minutes.
3. Divide rice pudding into bowls and serve.

4. Enjoy!

Nutrition: calories 251, fat 6, fiber 8, carbs 39, protein 12

24. Rustic Breakfast

Preparation time: 10 minutes **Cooking time:** 13 minutes **Servings:** 4

Ingredients:

- 7 ounces of baby spinach
- 8 chestnuts mushrooms, halved
- 8 tomatoes, halved
- 1 garlic clove, minced
- 4 chipolatas
- 4 bacon slices, chopped
- Salt and black pepper to the taste
- 4 eggs
- Cooking spray

Directions:

1. Grease a cooking pan with the oil and add tomatoes, garlic and mushrooms. Add the bacon and chipolata and spinach and broken eggs at the end.

2. Add salt and pepper, place the skillet in the frying pan and cook for 13 minutes at 350°F. Transfer to plates and serve. Enjoy!

Nutrition: calories 312, fat 6, fiber 8, carbs 15, protein 5

25. Shrimp Frittata

Preparation time: 17 minutes **Cooking time:** 15 minutes **Servings:** 4

Ingredients:

- 4 eggs
- ½ teaspoon basil, dried
- Cooking spray
- Salt and black pepper to the taste
- ½ cup rice, cooked
- ½ cup shrimp, cooked, peeled, deveined, and chopped
- ½ cup baby spinach, chopped
- ½ cup Monterey jack cheese, grated

Directions:

1. Mix eggs with salt, pepper and basil in a bowl and whisk.
2. Grease your Air Fryer's pan with cooking spray and add rice, shrimp and spinach.
3. Add eggs, mix, sprinkle cheese all over and cook in your Air Fryer at 350° F for 10 minutes.
4. Divide among plates and serve for breakfast.
5. Enjoy!

Nutrition: calories 162, fat 6, fiber 5, carbs 8, protein 4.

LUNCH-DINNER

26. Bacon and Garlic Pizzas

Preparation time: 10 minutes **Cooking time:** 10 minutes **Servings:** 4

Ingredients:

- 4 dinner rolls, frozen
- 4 garlic cloves minced
- ½ teaspoon oregano dried
- ½ teaspoon garlic powder
- 1 cup tomato sauce
- 8 bacon slices, cooked and chopped
- 1 and ¼ cups cheddar cheese, grated
- Cooking spray

Directions:

1. Place dinner rolls on a working surface and press them to obtain 4 ovals.
2. Spray each oval with cooking spray, transfer them to your Air Fryer.
3. Cook them at 370°F for 2 minutes.
4. Spread tomato sauce on each oval, divide garlic, sprinkle oregano and garlic powder and top with bacon and cheese.
5. Return pizzas to your heated Air Fryer and cook them at 370°F for 8 minutes more.
6. Serve them warm for lunch. Enjoy!

Nutrition: calories 217, fat 5, fiber 8, carbs 12, protein 4

27. Beef Cubes & Marjoram

Preparation time: 11 minutes **Cooking time:** 12 minutes **Servings:** 4

Ingredients:

- 1 pound sirloin, cubed
- 16 ounces jarred pasta sauce
- 1 and ½ cups breadcrumbs
- 2 tablespoons olive oil
- ½ teaspoon marjoram, dried
- White rice, already cooked for serving

Directions:

1. Mix beef cubes with pasta sauce and toss well.
2. In another bowl, mix the breadcrumbs with the marjoram and olive oil and mix well.
3. Soak the beef cubes in this mixture, place them in your deep fryer and cook 360 degrees F for 12 minutes.
4. Arrange on the plates and serve with white rice. Enjoy!

Nutrition: calories 272, fat 6, fiber 9, carbs 18, protein 12

28. Buttermilk Chicken Thighs

Preparation time: 13 minutes **Cooking time:** 18 minutes **Servings:** 4

Ingredients:

- 1 and ½ pounds chicken thighs
- 2 cups of buttermilk
- Salt and black pepper
- A pinch of cayenne pepper
- 2 cups of white flour
- 1 tbsp baking powder
- 1 tbsp sweet paprika
- 1 tbsp on garlic powder

Directions:

1. Mix chicken thighs with buttermilk, salt, pepper and cayenne.
2. Toss and leave aside for 6 hours.
3. In another bowl, mix flour and paprika, baking powder and garlic powder and stir.
4. Drain chicken thighs, dredge them into the flour mixture. Put them in the Air Fryer and cook at 360°F for 8 minutes.
5. Turn chicken pieces, cook them for another 10 minutes, place on a platter. Enjoy!

Nutrition: calories 202, fat 3, fiber 9, carbs 14, protein 5

29. Cheese Ravioli with Sauce

Preparation time: 18 minutes **Cooking time:** 8 minutes **Servings:** 6

Ingredients:

- 20 ounces of cheese ravioli
- 10 ounces of marinara sauce
- 1 tablespoon olive oil
- 1 cup of buttermilk
- 2 cups of breadcrumbs
- ¼ cup of Parmesan cheese, shredded

Directions:

1. Put the buttermilk in a bowl and the breadcrumbs in another.
2. Soak the ravioli in buttermilk, then in the breadcrumbs and place them in your fryer on a baking sheet. Sprinkle them with olive oil, bake at 400°F for 5 minutes.

3. Divide them on plates, sprinkle with Parmesan on top and serve for lunch. Enjoy!

Nutrition: calories 270, fat 12, fiber 6, carbs 30, protein 15

30. Chicken-corn Casserole

Preparation time: 11 minutes **Cooking time:** 30 minutes **Servings:** 6

Ingredients:

- 1 cup clean chicken broth
- 2 tsp garlic powder
- Salt and black pepper
- 6 ounces tinned coconut milk
- 1 and ½ cup of green lentils
- 2 pounds of skinless, boneless chicken breasts, cubed
- 1/3 cup cilantro, minced
- 3 cups of corn
- 3 handfuls of spinach
- 3 green onions, minced

Directions:

1. In a saucepan suitable for your air fryer, mix the stock with the coconut milk, salt, pepper, garlic powder, chicken, and lentils.
2. Add the corn, green onions, cilantro, and spinach, mix well, place in your fryer and bake at 350 degrees F for 30 minutes. Enjoy!

Nutrition: cal. 347, fat 12, fiber 10, carbs 20, prot 44

31. Chicken and Zucchini Mix

Preparation time: 12 minutes **Cooking time:** 20 minutes **Servings:** 4

Ingredients:

- 4 zucchinis, cut with a spiralizer
- 1 pound of chicken breasts, skinless, boneless and cubed
- 2 garlic cloves, minced
- 1 teaspoon olive oil
- Salt and black pepper

- 2 cups of cherry tomatoes, halved
- ½ cup of almonds, chopped

For the pesto:

- 2 cups basil
- 2 cups kale, chopped
- 1 tablespoon lemon juice
- 1 garlic clove
- ¾ cup of pine nuts
- ½ cup of olive oil
- A pinch of salt

Directions:

1. In a blender, mix the basil with the kale, lemon juice, garlic, pine nuts, olive oil and a springling of salt.
2. Heat a skillet suitable for your air fryer with the oil over medium heat, add the garlic, stir and cook for 1 minute.
3. Add the chicken, salt and pepper, stir, almonds, zucchini noodles, garlic, cherry tomatoes and pesto you did in the beginning. Stir gently, place in a pre-heated air fryer and cook at 360°F for 17 minutes.
4. Divide onto plates and serve. Enjoy!

Nutrition: calories 345, fat 8, fiber 7, carbs 12, protein 16

32. Chicken, Beans, Corn and Quinoa Casserole

Preparation time: 11 minutes **Cooking time:** 30 minutes **Servings**: 8

Ingredients:

- 1 cup quinoa, already cooked
- 3 cups chicken breast, cooked and shredded
- 14 ounces canned black beans
- 12 ounces corn
- ½ cup cilantro, chopped
- 6 kale leaves, chopped
- ½ cup green onions, chopped
- 1 cup clean tomato sauce
- 1 cup clean salsa
- 2 teaspoons chili powder

- 2 teaspoons cumin, ground
- 3 cups mozzarella cheese, shredded
- 1 tablespoon garlic powder
- Cooking spray
- 2 jalapeno peppers, chopped

Directions:

1. Spray a baking dish that fits your Air Fryer with cooking spray, add quinoa, chicken, black beans, corn, cilantro, kale, green onions, tomato sauce, salsa, chili powder, cumin, garlic powder, jalapenos and mozzarella.
2. Toss, introduce in your fryer and cook at 350°F for 17 minutes. Slice and serve warm.

Nutrition: calories 365, fat 12, fiber 6, crbs 22, protein 26

33. Chicken Breasts with Pepper & Mushrooms

Preparation time: 12 minutes Cooking time: 21 minutes **Servings:** 2

Ingredients:

- 3 orange bell peppers, cut in squares
- ¼ cup of honey
- 1/3 cup of soy sauce
- Salt and black pepper
- Cooking spray
- 6 mushrooms, cut into half
- 2 chicken breasts, skinless, deboned and coarsely cubed

Directions:

1. Mix the chicken with the salt, pepper, honey, soy sauce and a little cooking powder and mix well.
2. Thread chicken, peppers, and mushrooms onto skewers, put them in your fryer and cook at 338°F for 20 minutes. Spoon into plates and serve. Enjoy!

Nutrition: calories 262, fat 7, fiber 9, carbs 12, protein 6

34. Chicken Pie

Preparation time: 11 minutes **Cooking time:** 17 minutes **Servings:** 4

Ingredients:

- 2 chicken thighs, deboned, skinless and cut into pieces
- 1 carrot, minced
- 1 yellow onion, chopped
- 2 potatoes, minced
- 2 mushrooms, minced
- 1 teaspoon of soy sauce
- Salt and black pepper
- 1 teaspoon Italian seasoning
- ½ teaspoon of garlic powder
- 1 teaspoon Worcestershire sauce
- 1 tbsp flour
- 1 tbsp milk
- 2 puff pastry sheets
- 1 tablespoon of melted butter

Directions:

1. Heat a saucepan over medium-high heat, add the potatoes, carrots and onion, toss and cook for 2 minutes.
2. Add chicken and mushrooms, salt, soya sauce, pepper, Italian dressing, garlic powder, Worcestershire sauce, flour and milk.
3. Place 1 sheet of puff pastry on the bottom of your skillet and cut off the excess lip.
4. Add the chicken mixture, top with the other sheet of pastry. Cut off the excess and brush the cake with butter.
5. Put it in your fryer and cook at 360°F for 6 minutes. Allow the pie to cool, cut and serve.

Nutrition: calories 302, fat 5, fiber 7, carbs 14, protein 7

35. Chicken Salad

Preparation time: 9 minutes **Cooking time:** 19 minutes **Servings:** 4

Ingredients:

- 2 ears of corn, peeled
- 1 pound of chicken tenders, deboned
- Olive oil
- Salt and black pepper
- 1 teaspoon of sweet paprika
- 1 tablespoon brown sugar
- ½ teaspoon of garlic powder
- ½ iceberg lettuce head, cut in medium strips
- ½ romaine lettuce head, cut in medium strips
- 1 cup canned black beans, strained
- 1 cup cheddar cheese, grated
- 3 tablespoons cilantro, minced
- 4 green onions, minced
- 12 cherry tomatoes, sliced
- ¼ cup of ranch dressing
- 3 tablespoons of BBQ sauce

Directions:

1. Put the corn in your air fryer, pour some oil and toss. Cook at 400°F for 10 minutes, place on a plate and reserve.
2. Add the chicken to your basket Air Fryer, add the salt, pepper, brown sugar, paprika and garlic powder, stir. Pour a little more oil, cook at 400°F for 10 minutes, turning them halfway. Move the tenders onto a cutting board and chop them.
3. Remove kernels from the cob, transfer corn into a bowl. Incorporate chicken, iceberg lettuce, romaine lettuce, black beans, cheese, coriander, tomatoes, onions, BBQ sauce and ranch dressing. Mix well and serve.
4. Enjoy!

Nutrition: calories 373, fat 6, fiber 9, carbs 17, protein 6

36. Chicken Sandwiches

Preparation time: 11 minutes **Cooking time:** 10 minutes **Servings:** 4

Ingredients:

- 2 chicken breasts, skinless, boneless and cubed
- 1 red onion, chopped
- 1 red bell pepper, sliced
- ½ cup Italian seasoning
- ½ teaspoon thyme, dried
- 2 cups butter lettuce, torn
- 4 pita pockets
- 1 cup cherry tomatoes, halved
- 1 tablespoon olive oil

Directions:

1. In your Air Fryer, mix chicken with onion, bell pepper, Italian seasoning and oil and toss. Cook at 380°F for 10 minutes.
2. Transfer chicken mix to a bowl, add thyme, butter lettuce and cherry tomatoes, toss well, stuff pita pockets with this mix and serve.

Nutrition: calories 126, fat 4, fiber 8, carbs 14, protein 4

37. Chinese Pork Lunch

Preparation time: 14 minutes **Cooking time:** 13 minutes **Servings:** 4

Ingredients:

- 2 eggs
- 2 pounds of pork, cut in medium cubes
- 1 cup of cornstarch

- 1 teaspoon of sesame oil
- Salt and black pepper
- A pinch of Chinese five spice
- 3 tablespoons of canola oil
- Sweet tomato sauce to serve

Directions:

1. Mix the 5 spices with the salt, pepper and cornstarch and mix well. In a separate bowl, combine the eggs with the sesame oil and beat well.
2. Wash the pork cubes in the cornstarch mixture, then dip them in the egg mixture and put them in your fryer that you greased with the canola oil. Bake at 340°F for 12 minutes, shaking the fryer once.
3. Serve pork with the sweet tomato sauce on the side. Enjoy!

Nutrition: calories 322, fat 8, fiber 12, carbs 20, protein 5

38. Coconut and Chicken Breast Casserole

Preparation time: 10 minutes **Cooking time:** 26 minutes **Servings:** 4

Ingredients:

- 4 lime leaves, shredded
- 1 cup of veggie broth
- 1 lemongrass stalk, minced
- 1 inch piece, shredded
- 1 pound chicken breast, skin-free, deboned, cut into thin strips
- 8 ounces of mushrooms, minced
- 4 Thai chilies, minced
- 4 tablespoons of fish sauce
- 6 ounces of coconut milk
- ¼ cup of lime juice
- ¼ cup cilantro, minced
- Salt and black pepper

Directions:

1. Place the broth in a skillet suitable for your air fryer, bring to simmer over medium heat. Add the lemon grass, ginger and lime leaves, toss and cook for 10 minutes.
2. Drain the soup and return to the pan. Add the chicken, mushrooms, milk, chilies, the fish sauce, lime juice, cilantro, salt and pepper and stir.
3. Put in your air fryer and cook at 360° F for 15 minutes. Arrange in bowls and serve. Enjoy!

Nutrition: calories 152, fat 4, fiber 4, carbs 6, protein 7

39. Corn and Swiss Cheese Casserole

Preparation time: 9 minutes **Cooking time:** 16 minutes **Servings:** 4

Ingredients:

- 2 cups of corn
- 3 tbsp of flour
- 1 egg
- ¼ cup of milk
- ½ cup of light cream
- ½ cup of Swiss cheese, grated
- 2 tbsp of butter
- Salt and black pepper
- Cooking spray

Directions:

1. Mix the corn with flour, egg, milk, light cream, Swiss cheese, salt, pepper and butter and blend well.
2. Grease your Air Fryer skillet with cooking spray, pour the cream mixture, spread out and cook at 320°F for 15 minutes. Serve warm. Enjoy!

Nutrition: calories 282, fat 7, fiber 8, carbs 9, protein 6

40. Creamy Chicken Stew

Preparation time: 11 minutes **Cooking time:** 24 minutes **Servings:** 4

Ingredients:

- 1 and ½ cups creamy canned celery soup
- 6 chicken tenders
- Salt and black pepper
- 2 potatoes, chopped
- 1 bay leaf
- 1 thyme spring, minced
- 1 tablespoon of milk
- 1 egg yolk
- ½ cup of heavy cream

Directions:

1. Blend the chicken with the celery cream, potatoes, thick cream, bay leaf, thyme, salt and pepper.
2. Place in your frying pan and bake at 320 degrees F for 25 minutes.
3. Let cool slightly, discard the bay leaf, place in the plates and serve immediately. Enjoy!

Nutrition: calories 304, fat 11, fiber 2, carbs 23, protein 14

41. Easy Chicken Shiitake Mushrooms

Preparation time: 14 minutes **Cooking time:** 21 minutes **Servings:** 6

Ingredients:

- 1 bunch kale, chopped
- Salt and black pepper to the taste
- ¼ cup chicken stock
- 1 cup chicken, shredded
- 3 carrots, chopped
- 1 cup shiitake mushrooms, roughly sliced

Directions:

1. In a blender, mix the broth with the kale, mix a few times and pour into a pan which adapts to your fryer.
2. Stir in chicken, mushrooms, carrots, salt and pepper to taste. Introduce into your air fryer and cook at 350°F for 18 minutes. Enjoy!

Nutrition: calories 183, fat 7 fiber 2, carbs 10, protein 5

42. Hash Brown Toasts

Preparation time: 9 minutes **Cooking time:** 8 minutes Servings: 4

Ingredients:

- four hash brown patties, frozen
- 1 tablespoon of olive oil
- ¼ cup cherry tomatoes, minced
- 3 tablespoons mozzarella, shredded
- 2 tbsp of Parmesan, grated
- 1 tbsp balsamic vinegar
- 1 tbsp basil, minced

Directions:

1. Place hash browns in your fryer, sprinkle with oil and cook at 400 degrees F for 7 minutes.
2. Toss tomatoes with mozzarella, Parmesan, vinegar and basil and mix well.
3. Spoon hash brown patties on plates, top each with tomato mix and serve. Enjoy!

Nutrition: calories 200, fat 3, fiber 8, carbs 12, protein 4

43. Hot Bacon Sandwiches

Preparation time: 12 minutes **Cooking time:** 9 minutes

Servings: 4

Ingredients:

- 1/3 cup of BBQ sauce
- 2 tablespoons of honey

- 8 slices of bacon, cooked and quartered
- 1 red bell pepper, sliced
- 1 yellow bell pepper, sliced
- 3 pita pockets, cut in half
- 1 and ¼ cup of butter lettuce leaves, torn
- 2 tomatoes, chopped

Directions:

1. Mix the BBQ sauce with honey and toss well. Coat bacon and all bell peppers with some of this mix. Put them in your air fryer and bake at 350 degrees F for 4 minutes.
2. Shake the fryer and cook an extra 2 minutes. Stuff the pita pockets with the bacon mixture, fill with the tomatoes and lettuce, and spread the rest of the BBQ sauce. Serve. Enjoy!

Nutrition: calories 188, fat 6, fiber 9, carbs 14, protein 4

44. Italian Eggplant Sandwich

Preparation time: 14 minutes **Cooking time:** 17 minutes **Servings:** 2

Ingredients:

- 1 eggplant, sliced
- 2 teaspoons parsley, chopped
- Salt and black pepper
- ½ cup of breadcrumbs
- ½ teaspoon Italian seasoning
- ½ teaspoon garlic powder
- ½ teaspoon onion powder
- 2 tablespoons of milk
- 4 bread slices
- Cooking spray
- ½ cup of mayonnaise

- ¾ cup tomato sauce
- 2 cups grated mozzarella cheese

Directions:

1. Add salt and pepper to the eggplant slices, leave aside for 10 minutes, then dry well. Combine parsley, breadcrumbs, Italian seasoning, onion and garlic powder, salt and black pepper and stir.
2. In another bowl, mix milk with mayo and whisk well.
3. Brush eggplant slices with mayo mix, dip them in breadcrumbs, place them in your Air Fryer's basket, spray with cooking oil and cook them at 400°F for 15 minutes, flipping them after 8 minutes.
4. Brush each bread slice with olive oil and arrange 2 on a working surface. Add mozzarella and parmesan on each, add baked eggplant slices, spread tomato sauce and basil and top with the other bread slices, greased side down.
5. Divide sandwiches on plates cut them in halves and serve. Enjoy!

Nutrition: calories 324, fat 16, fiber 4, carbs 39, protein 12

45. Japanese Chicken Mix

Preparation time: 10 minutes **Cooking time:** 8 minutes **Servings:** 2

Ingredients:

- 2 chicken thighs, skinless and boneless
- 2 ginger slices, chopped
- 3 garlic cloves, minced
- ¼ cup soy sauce
- ¼ cup mirin
- 1/8 cup's sake
- ½ teaspoon sesame oil
- 1/8 cup water
- 2 tablespoons sugar
- 1 tablespoon cornstarch mixed with 2 tablespoons water
- Sesame seeds for serving

Directions:

1. In a bowl, mix chicken thighs with ginger, garlic, soy sauce, mirin, sake, oil, water, sugar and cornstarch, toss well, transfer to preheated Air Fryer, cook at 360°F for 8 minutes.
2. Transfer to the plates, sprinkle with sesame seeds and serve with a side salad. Enjoy!

Nutrition: calories 300, fat 7, fiber 9, carbs 17, protein 10

46. Lentils Fritters

Preparation time: 15 minutes **Cooking time:** 13 minutes **Servings:** 2

Ingredients:

- 1 cup yellow lentils, soaked in water for 1 hour and drained
- 1 hot chili pepper, chopped
- 1 inch ginger piece, grated
- ½ teaspoon turmeric powder
- 1 teaspoon garam masala
- 1 teaspoon baking powder
- Salt and black pepper to the taste
- 2 teaspoons olive oil
- 1/3 cup water
- ½ cup cilantro, chopped
- 1 and ½ cup spinach, chopped
- 4 garlic cloves, minced
- ¾ cup red onion, chopped
- Mint chutney for serving

Directions:

1. In your blender, mix lentils with chili pepper, ginger, turmeric, garam masala, baking powder, salt, pepper, olive oil, water, cilantro, spinach, onion and garlic.
2. Blend well and shape medium balls out of this mix.
3. Place them all in your preheated Air Fryer at 400 degrees F and cook for 10 minutes.
4. Serve your veggie fritters with a side salad for lunch. Enjoy!

Nutrition: calories 142, fat 2, fiber 8, carbs 12, protein 4

47. Sweet Potato Lunch Casserole

Preparation time: 10 minutes **Cooking time:** 50 minutes **Servings:** 6

Ingredients:

- 3 big, sweet potatoes, pricked with a fork
- 1 cup chicken stock
- Salt and black pepper to the taste
- A pinch of cayenne pepper
- ¼ teaspoon nutmeg, ground
- 1/3 cup coconut cream

Directions:

1. Place sweet potatoes in your Air Fryer, cook them at 350°F for 40 minutes, cool them down, peel, roughly chop.
2. Transfer to a pan that fits your Air Fryer.
3. Add stock, salt, pepper, cayenne and coconut cream, toss.
4. Introduce in your Air Fryer, cook at 360°F for 10 minutes more.
5. Divide casserole into bowls and serve. Enjoy!

Nutrition: calories 245, fat 4, fiber 5, carbs 10, protein 6

48. Tasty Cheeseburgers

Preparation time: 9 minutes **Cooking time:** 22 minutes **Servings:** 2

Ingredients:

- 12 ounces lean beef, ground
- 4 teaspoons ketchup
- 3 tablespoons yellow onion, chopped
- 2 teaspoons mustard
- Salt and black pepper to the taste
- 4 cheddar cheese slices
- 2 burger buns, halved

Directions:

2. In a bowl, mix beef with onion, ketchup, mustard, salt and pepper, stir well and shape 4 patties out of this mix.
3. Divide cheese on 2 patties and top with the other 2 patties.
4. Place them in preheated Air Fryer at 370 degrees F and fry them for 20 minutes.
5. Divide cheeseburger on 2 bun halves, top with the other 2 and serve for lunch.
6. Enjoy!

Nutrition: calories 261, fat 6, fiber 10, carbs 20, protein 6

SIDE DISHES

49. Air Fried Creamy Cabbage

Preparation time: 12 minutes **Cooking time:** 20 minutes **Servings:** 4

Ingredients:

- 1 green cabbage head, minced
- 1 yellow onion, minced
- Salt and black pepper to the taste
- 4 bacon slices, minced
- 1 cup of whipped cream
- 2 tablespoons of cornstarch

Directions:

1. Place the cabbage, bacon and onion in your Air Fryer. Mix the cornstarch cream, salt and pepper, stir and add the kale.
2. Stir, cook at 400 degrees F for 20 minutes, place on plates and serve. Enjoy!

Nutrition: calories 209, fat 10, fiber 3, carbs 16, protein 5

50. Artichokes and Tarragon Sauce

Preparation time: 15 minutes **Cooking time:** 19 minutes **Servings:** 4

Ingredients:

- 4 artichokes, trimmed
- 2 tablespoons tarragon, chopped
- 2 tablespoons chicken stock
- Lemon zest from 2 lemons, grated
- 2 tablespoons lemon juice
- 1 celery stalk, chopped
- ½ cup olive oil
- Salt to the taste

Directions:

1. Mix the tarragon, chicken stock, lemon peel, lemon juice, celery, salt and olive oil in your food processor.
2. Blend artichokes with tarragon and lemon sauce, mix well and transfer to your Air Fryer basket, cook at 380°F for 19 minutes.
3. Place the artichokes on the plates, sprinkle with the sauce and serve. Enjoy!

Nutrition: calories 216, fat 3, fiber 8, carbs 28, protein 6

51. Cajun Onion Wedges with Paprika

Preparation time: 13 minutes **Cooking time:** 15 minutes **Servings:** 4

Ingredients:

- 2 big white onions, cut into wedges
- Salt and black pepper to the taste
- 2 eggs
- ¼ cup milk
- 1/3 cup panko
- A drizzle of olive oil
- 1 and ½ teaspoon paprika
- 1 teaspoon garlic powder
- ½ teaspoon Cajun seasoning

Directions:

1. Blend panko with Cajun seasoning and oil and toss.
2. Mix egg with milk, salt, and pepper in another bowl, stir.

3. Sprinkle the onions with the paprika and garlic powder, dip them in the egg mixture, then in the breadcrumbs. Put them in your Air Fryer basket, cook at 360°F for 13 minutes, turn them over and cook for another 5 minutes.
4. Divide among plates and serve. Enjoy!

Nutrition: calories 202, fat 2, fiber 2, carbs 14, protein 7

52. Carrots and Rhubarb

Preparation time: 9 minutes **Cooking time:** 42 minutes **Servings:** 4

Ingredients:

- 1 pound of baby carrots
- 2 teaspoons of walnut oil
- 1 pound rhubarb, roughly cut
- 1 orange, peeled (cut it into medium segments and zest grated)
- ½ cup of walnuts, halved
- ½ teaspoon of stevia

Directions:

1. Place the oil in your air fryer, add the carrots and sauté at 380 degrees F for 20 minutes.
2. Add the rhubarb, orange peel, stevia, and walnuts, mix and cook for another 22 minutes. Stir in the orange wedges and serve. Enjoy!

Nutrition: calories 173, fat 2, fiber 3, carbs 4, protein 5.

53. Cauliflower and Broccoli

Preparation time: 14 minutes **Cooking time:** 8 minutes **Servings:** 4

Ingredients:

- 2 cauliflower heads (separate florets and steam)
- 1 broccoli head, (separate florets and steam)
- Zest from 1 orange

- Grated Juice from 1 orange
- A pinch of hot pepper flakes
- 4 anchovies
- 1 tablespoon capers, chopped
- Salt and black pepper to the taste
- 4 tablespoons olive oil

Directions:

1. Blend the orange peel with the orange juice, pepper flakes, anchovies, caper salt, pepper and olive oil, whisk well.
2. Add broccoli and cauliflower, mix well, transfer them to your air fryer basket. Bake at 400°F for 7 minutes. Spoon into plates and serve as an accompaniment with a drizzle of orange vinaigrette. Enjoy!

Nutrition: calories 302, fat 4, fiber 7, carbs 28, protein 5

54. Cauliflower Cakes with Parmesan

Preparation time: 10 minutes **Cooking time:** 10 minutes **Servings:** 6

Ingredients:

- 3 and ½ cups cauliflower rice
- 2 eggs
- ¼ cup white flour
- ½ cup Parmesan, grated
- Salt and black pepper to the taste
- Cooking spray

Directions:

1. Mix the cauliflower rice with salt and pepper, stir and squeeze the excess water.
2. Transfer the cauliflower into another bowl, add the eggs, salt, pepper, flour and Parmesan, mix well and shape your cakes.
3. Grease your fryer with cooking spray, heat it to 400 degrees, add cauliflower cakes and cook for 10 minutes, turning halfway.
4. Serve. Enjoy!

Nutrition: calor 126, fat 2, fiber 6, carbs 8, protein 3

55. Cauliflower Rice

Preparation time: 11 minutes **Cooking time:** 40 minutes **Servings:** 8

Ingredients:

- 1 tablespoon of peanut oil
- 1 tablespoon sesame oil
- 4 tablespoons of soy sauce
- 3 garlic cloves, minced
- 1 tablespoon ginger, grated
- Juice from ½ lemon
- 1 cauliflower head, riced
- 9 ounces of water chestnuts, dripped
- ¾ cup of peas
- 15 ounces sliced mushrooms
- 1 egg, whipped

Directions:

1. In your air fryer, blend the cauliflower rice with the peanut oil, sesame oil, soya sauce, garlic, ginger and lemon juice.
2. Cover it and bake at 350°F for 20 minutes. Add the chestnuts, peas, mushrooms, and egg, stir and cook at 360 degrees F for 20 minutes.
3. Divide among plates and serve. Enjoy!

Nutrition: calories 143, fat 3, fiber 2, carbs 6, protein 4

56. Cheddar Biscuits

Preparation time: 13 minutes **Cooking time:** 20 minutes **Servings:** 8

Ingredients:

- 2 and 1/3 cup self-rising flour
- ½ cup butter+ 1 tablespoon, melted
- 2 tablespoons sugar
- ½ cup cheddar cheese, grated
- 1 and 1/3 cup buttermilk
- 1 cup flour

Directions:

1. Mix the self-rising flour with ½ cup of butter, sugar, cheddar cheese and buttermilk and toss until obtain a paste.
2. Spread 1 cup of flour on a work surface, roll up the dough, flatten, cut 8 circles with a cookie cutter and coat with flour.
3. Line your Air Fryer basket with foil, add the cookies, brush them with melted butter and bake them at 380 degrees F for 20 minutes.
4. Divide among plates and serve.
5. Enjoy!

Nutrition: calories 222, fat 3, fiber 8, carbs 12, protein 4

57. Coconut Cream Potatoes

Preparation time: 16 minutes **Cooking time:** 20 minutes **Servings:** 4

Ingredients:

- 2 eggs, whisked
- Salt and black pepper to the taste
- 1 tablespoon cheddar cheese, grated
- 1 tablespoon flour
- 2 potatoes, sliced
- 4 ounces of coconut cream

Directions:

1. Add potato slices to the Air Fryer and bake at 360°F for 10 minutes. Blend the eggs with the coconut cream, salt, pepper and flour.
2. Put the potatoes in your Air Fryer pan, add the coconut cream, sprinkle the cheese, return to the Air Fryer and bake them 10 minutes at 400°F for 10.
3. Divide among plates and serve.
4. Enjoy!

Nutrition: calories 171, fat 4, fiber 1, carbs 15, protein 17

58. Colored Veggie Rice

Preparation time: 16 minutes **Cooking time:** 25 minutes **Servings**: 4

Ingredients:

- 2 cups of basmati rice
- 1 cup of mixed carrots, peas, corn and green beans
- 2 cups water
- ½ teaspoon green chili, minced
- ½ teaspoon ginger, grated
- 3 garlic cloves, minced
- 2 tablespoons butter
- 1 teaspoon cinnamon powder
- 1 tablespoon cumin seeds
- 2 bay leaves
- 3 whole cloves
- 5 black peppercorns
- 2 whole cardamoms
- 1 tablespoon sugar
- Salt to the taste

Directions:

1. Place the water into a heat-resistant container on your fryer. Add rice, mixed vegetables, chili pepper, grated ginger, garlic, cloves, cinnamon, butter, cumin seeds, bay leaves, cardamom, black pepper, salt and salted sugar, stir.
2. Put into your fryer basket and bake at 370°F for 25 minutes.
3. Divide among plates and serve. Enjoy!

Nutrition: calories 284, fat 4, fiber 8, carbs 34, protein 14

59. Corn with Lime and Cheese

Preparation time: 10 minutes **Cooking time:** 15 minutes **Servings:** 2

Ingredients:

- 2 corns on the cob, peeled off
- A drizzle of olive oil
- ½ cup of feta cheese, grated
- 2 teaspoons of sweet paprika
- Juice from 2 limes

Directions:

1. Rub the corn with the oil and paprika, put it in your fryer and bake at 400 degrees F for 15 minutes, turning once.
2. Spread the corn on the plates, sprinkle with cheese, drizzle with lime juice. Enjoy!

Nutrition: calories 201, fat 5, fiber 2, carbs 6, prot 7

60. Creamy Air Fried Potatos

Preparation time: 13 minutes **Cooking time:** 1 hour and 20 minutes **Servings:**2

Ingredients:

- 1 big potato
- 2 bacon strips, cooked and chopped
- 1 teaspoon olive oil
- 1/3 cup cheddar cheese, shredded
- 1 tablespoon green onions, chopped
- Salt and black pepper to the taste
- 1 tablespoon butter
- 2 tablespoons heavy cream

Directions:

1. Rub the potatoes with the oil, season with salt and pepper, put them in the pre-heated air fryer and bake at 400 degrees F for 30 minutes.
2. Turn potatoes upside down, cook for another 30 minutes, place on a cutting board, cool, cut in half lengthwise and divide in a bowl.
3. Add the bacon, cheese, butter, the heavy cream, green onions, salt and pepper. Mix well and fill the potato skins with this mixture. Return the potatoes to your fryer and bake them at 400°F for 20 minutes.
4. Divide among plates and serve. Enjoy!

Nutrition: calories 173, fat 5, fiber 7, carbs 9, prot 4

61. Creamy Brussels Sprouts

Preparation time: 14 minutes **Cooking time:** 25 minutes **Servings:** 8

Ingredients:

- 3 pounds Brussels sprouts, halved
- A drizzle of olive oil
- 1 pound bacon, chopped
- Salt and black pepper to the taste
- 4 tablespoons butter
- 3 shallots, chopped
- 1 cup milk
- 2 cups heavy cream
- ¼ teaspoon nutmeg, ground
- 3 tablespoons prepared horseradish

Directions:

1. Preheat your air fryer to 370°F. Add the oil, bacon, salt and pepper and Brussels sprouts and blend.
2. Add butter, scallions, heavy cream, milk, nutmeg, and horseradish, stir and cook for 25 minutes.
3. Divide among plates and serve. Enjoy!

Nutrition: calories 215, fat 5, fiber 8, carbs 12, protein 5

62. Creamy Endives with Greek Yogurt

Preparation time: 12 minutes **Cooking time:** 10 minutes **Servings:** 6

Ingredients:

- 6 endives, dressed and cut in two
- 1 teaspoon of garlic powder
- ½ cup of Greek yogurt
- ½ teaspoon of curry powder
- Salt and black pepper
- 3 tablespoons of lemon juice

Directions:

1. Combine the endives with the garlic powder, yoghurt, curry powder, salt, pepper and lemon juice. Set aside for 10 minutes and transfer to your preheated 350°F fryer.
2. Bake the endives for 10 minutes, divide them into plates and serve. Enjoy!

Nutrition: calories 102, fat 2, fiber 2, carbs 7, prot 5

63. Creamy Potatoes

Preparation time: 11 minutes **Cooking time:** 20 minutes **Servings:** 4

Ingredients:

- 1 and ½ pounds of potatoes, peeled and cubed
- 2 tablespoons of olive oil
- Salt and black pepper
- 1 tablespoon of hot paprika
- 1 cup of Greek yogurt

Directions:

1. Put the potatoes into a bowl, add the water to cover, set aside for 10 minutes, drain, pat dry. Transfer to a separate bowl, add salt, pepper, paprika and half the oil and mix well. Place the potatoes into your Air Fryer basket and bake at 360°F for 20 minutes.
2. Mix yogurt with salt, pepper, and oil and whisk.
3. Divide potatoes among plates, drizzle yogurt dressing, toss them and serve. Enjoy!

Nutrition: calories 171, fat 3, fiber 5, carbs 20, protein 5

64. Creamy Roasted Pepper

Preparation time: 9 minutes **Cooking time:** 10 minutes **Servings:** 4

Ingredients:

- 1 tablespoon of lemon juice
- 1 red bell pepper
- 1 green bell pepper
- 1 yellow bell pepper
- 1 lettuce head, cut into strips
- 1 ounce of rocket leaves
- Salt and black pepper
- 3 tablespoons of Greek yogurt
- 2 tablespoons of olive oil

Directions:

1. Place the peppers in your Air Fryer basket, cook at 400°F for 10 minutes. Put in a bowl, reserve 10 minutes, peel, discard the seeds and cut into strips.
2. Transfer to larger bowl, add arugula leaves and strips of lettuce and stir to combine. Blend the oil with the lemon juice, yoghurt, salt and pepper and whisk well.
3. Add to the bell pepper mix, toss to coat, divide among the plates and serve as.
4. Enjoy!

Nutrition: calories 171, fat 1, fiber 1, carbs 2, protein 6

65. Crispy Brussels Sprouts with Potatoes

Preparation time: 14 minutes **Cooking time:** 8 minutes **Servings:** 4

Ingredients:

- 1 and ½ pounds of Brussels sprouts, washed and dressed
- 1 cup of new potatoes, chopped
- 1 and ½ tablespoons of breadcrumbs
- Salt and black pepper
- 1 and ½ tablespoons of butter

Directions:

1. Put the Brussels sprouts and potatoes in your skillet, add the breadcrumbs, salt, pepper and butter, mix well and cook at 400°F for 8 minutes.
2. Spoon onto plates and serve. Enjoy!

Nutrition: calories 153, fat 3, fiber 7, carbs 17, protein 4

66. Delicious Air Fried Broccoli

Preparation time: 14 minutes **Cooking time:** 20 minutes **Servings:** 4

Ingredients:

- 1 tablespoon duck fat
- 1 broccoli head, florets separated
- 3 garlic cloves, minced
- Juice from ½ lemon
- 1 tablespoon sesame seeds

Directions:

1. Heat your air fryer to 350°F. Stir in duck fat and heat through. Add the broccoli, garlic, lemon juice and sesame seeds and mix. Simmer for 20 minutes.
2. Divide among plates and serve. Enjoy!

Nutrition: calories 133, fat 3, fiber 3, carbs 6, protein 5

67. Delicious Roasted Carrots

Preparation time: 13 minutes **Cooking time:** 20 minutes **Servings:** 4

Ingredients:

- 1 pound of baby carrots
- 2 teaspoons of olive oil
- 1 teaspoon of herbs de Provence
- 4 tablespoons orange juice

Directions:

1. Mix carrots with Provencal herbs, oil and orange juice in your Air Fryer basket, mix and bake at 320°F for 20 minutes.
2. Divide among plates and serve. Enjoy!

Nutrition: calories 113, fat 2, fiber 3, carbs 4, prot 4

68. Garlic Potatoes

Preparation time: 9 minutes **Cooking time:** 20 minutes **Servings:** 6

Ingredients:

- 2 tablespoons parsley, chopped
- 5 garlic cloves, minced
- ½ teaspoon basil, dried
- ½ teaspoon oregano, dried
- 3 pounds red potatoes, halved
- 1 teaspoon thyme, dried
- 2 tablespoons olive oil
- Salt and black pepper to the taste
- 2 tablespoons butter
- 1/3 cup parmesan, grated

Directions:

1. Blend the potato halves with the parsley, garlic, basil, oregano, thyme, salt and pepper, oil and butter.
2. Cover it and bake at 400°F for 20 minutes, turning once. Sprinkle with Parmesan cheese, place the potatoes on the plates and serve as a side dish. Enjoy!

Nutrition: calories 163, fat 5, fiber 5, carbs 7, prot 5

69. Glazed Beets

Preparation time: 8 minutes **Cooking time:** 40 minutes **Servings:** 8

Ingredients:

- 3 pounds small beets, trimmed
- 4 tablespoons maple syrup
- 1 tablespoon duck fat

Directions:

1. Heat your fryer to 360° F, add the duck fat and heat it. Stir in beets and maple syrup and cook for 40 minutes.
2. Divide among plates and serve. Enjoy!

Nutrition: calories 122, fat 3, fiber 2, carbs 3, prot 4

70. Pumpkin Rice

Preparation time: 6 minutes **Cooking time:** 30 minutes **Servings:** 4

Ingredients:

- 2 tablespoons olive oil
- 1 small yellow onion, chopped
- 2 garlic cloves, minced
- 12 ounces of white rice
- 4 cups chicken stock
- 6 ounces of pumpkin puree
- ½ teaspoon nutmeg
- 1 teaspoon thyme, chopped
- ½ teaspoon ginger, grated
- ½ teaspoon cinnamon powder
- ½ teaspoon allspice
- 4 ounces of heavy cream

Directions:

1. In a dish that suits your fryer, mix the oil with the onion, garlic, rice, broth, pumpkin purée, nutmeg, thyme, ginger, cinnamon, Jamaican pepper and cream.

2. Mix well, place in your fryer basket and bake at 360°F for 30 minutes.
3. Divide among plates and serve. Enjoy!

Nutrition: calories 262, fat 6, fiber 7, carbs 29, protein 4

71. Rice and Sausage

Preparation time: 12 minutes **Cooking time:** 20 minutes **Servings:** 4

Ingredients:

- 2 cups white rice, already boiled
- 1 tablespoon butter
- Salt and black pepper to the taste
- 4 garlic cloves, minced
- 1 pork sausage, chopped
- 2 tablespoons carrot, chopped
- 3 tablespoons cheddar cheese, grated
- 2 tablespoons mozzarella cheese, shredded

Directions:

1. Warm your air fryer to 350 degrees F, add the butter, melt it, add the garlic, stir and cook for 2 minutes. Add sausages, salt, pepper, carrots and rice, mix and bake at 350°F for 10 minutes.
2. Add the cheddar and mozzarella cheese, mix, divide and serve as a side dish.
3. Enjoy!

Nutrition: calories 241, fat 12, fiber 5, carbs 20, protein 13

72. Roasted Eggplant

Preparation time: 9 minutes **Cooking time:** 20 minutes **Servings:** 6

Ingredients:

- 1 and ½ pounds of cubed eggplant
- 1 tablespoon of olive oil
- 1 teaspoon of garlic powder
- 1 teaspoon of onion powder
- 1 teaspoon of sumac
- 2 teaspoons of za'atar
- Juice from ½ lemon
- 2 bay leaves

Directions:

1. In your fryer, mix the eggplant cubes with the oil, garlic powder, onion powder, sumac, za'atar, lemon juice and laurel leaves.
2. Bake on 370°F for 20 minutes. Divide among plates and serve.
3. Enjoy!

Nutrition: calories 174, fat 4, fiber 7, carbs 12, protein 3

SNACKS & APPETIZERS

73. Air Fried Dill Pickles

Preparation time: 9 minutes **Cooking time:** 5 minutes **Servings:** 4

Ingredients:

- 16 ounces canned dill pickles, quartered and drained
- ½ cup of white flour
- 1 egg
- ¼ cup of milk
- ½ teaspoon of garlic powder
- ½ teaspoon of sweet paprika
- Cooking spray
- ¼ cup of ranch sauce

Directions:

1. Combine milk with egg and whisk well.
2. Mix flour salt, garlic powder, and paprika in a second bowl and stir.
3. Dip the pickles in flour, then in the egg mixture and again in flour. Place them in your air fryer.
4. Grease them with cooking spray, cook them at 400°F for 5 minutes. Transfer into a bowl and serve them with ranch sauce on the side. Enjoy!

Nutrition: calories 110, fat 2, fiber 2, carbs 10, protein 4

74. Beef Party Rolls

Preparation time: 16 minutes **Cooking time:** 15 minutes **Servings:** 4

Ingredients:

- 14 ounces of beef stock
- 7 ounces white wine
- 4 beef cutlets
- Salt and black pepper to the taste
- 8 sage leaves
- 4 ham slices
- 1 tablespoon butter, melted

Directions:

1. Heat a pan with the stock over medium-high, add wine and cook until it reduces, take off the heat and divide into small bowls.
2. Salt and pepper the cutlets, cover with sage, and roll each into strips of ham.
3. Brush the rolls with butter, put them in your Air Fryer's basket and bake at 400°F for 15 minutes.
4. Place the rolls on a tray and serve with the dressing on the side. Enjoy!

Nutrition: calories 262, fat 12, fiber 1, carbs 22, protein 21

75. Beef Patties

Preparation time: 11 minutes **Cooking time:** 8 minutes **Servings:** 4

Ingredients:

- 14 ounces beef, minced
- 2 tablespoons ham, cut into strips
- 1 leek, chopped
- 3 tablespoons breadcrumbs
- Salt and black pepper to the taste
- ½ teaspoon nutmeg, ground

Directions:

1. Mix beef with leek, salt, pepper, ham, breadcrumbs, and nutmeg, stir well and shape small patties out of this mix.
2. Place them in your Air Fryer's basket, bake at 400°F for 8 minutes. Put them on a platter and serve as an appetizer. Enjoy!

Nutrition: calories 260, fat 12, fiber 3, carbs 12, protein 21

76. Beef Rolls

Preparation time: 16 minutes **Cooking time:** 15 minutes **Servings:** 4

Ingredients:

- 2 pounds of beef steak, open and flat with a meat tenderizer
- Salt and black pepper
- 1 cup of baby spinach
- 3 ounces red bell pepper, roasted and minced
- 6 slices of provolone cheese
- 3 tablespoons pesto

Directions:

1. Place the flat beef steak on a cutting board, spread the pesto throughout, add the cheese in a single layer and add the peppers, spinach, salt and pepper to taste.
2. Roll your steak, secure it with toothpicks, season again with salt and pepper, place the roll in your Air Fryer's basket.
3. Cook at 400°F for 14 minutes, rotating the roll halfway. Leave aside to cool down, cut into 2-inch smaller rolls.
4. Arrange on a platter and serve. Enjoy!

Nutrition: calories 231, fat 1, fiber 3, carbs 12, protein 10

77. Broccoli Patties

Preparation time: 13 minutes **Cooking time:** 10 minutes **Servings:** 12

Ingredients:

- 4 cups broccoli florets
- 1 and ½ cup almond flour
- 1 teaspoon paprika
- Salt and black pepper to the taste
- 2 eggs
- ¼ cup olive oil
- 2 cups cheddar cheese, grated
- 1 teaspoon garlic powder
- ½ teaspoon apple cider vinegar
- ½ teaspoon baking soda

Directions:

1. Put broccoli florets in your food processor, add salt and pepper, blend well and transfer to a bowl.
2. Add almond flour, salt, pepper, paprika, garlic powder, baking soda, cheese, oil, eggs and vinegar, stir well and shape 12 patties out of this mix.
3. Place them in your preheated Air Fryer's basket and bake at 350 degrees F for 10 minutes.
4. Arrange patties on a platter and serve. Enjoy!

Nutrition: calories 203, fat 12, fiber 2, carbs 14, protein 2

78. Buffalo Cauliflower

Preparation time: 9 minutes **Cooking time:** 15 minutes **Servings:** 4

Ingredients:

- 4 cups cauliflower florets
- 1 cup panko breadcrumbs
- ¼ cup butter, melted
- ¼ cup buffalo sauce
- Mayonnaise for serving

Directions:

1. Combine the buffalo sauce with the butter and whisk thoroughly. Dip the cauliflower florets into the mixture and coat them with panko breadcrumbs. Put them in the basket of your air fryer and bake at 350 degrees F for 15 minutes.
2. Lay them on a tray and serve them with the mayonnaise on the side. Enjoy!

Nutrition: calories 242, fat 4, fiber 7, carbs 8, prot 5

79. Cajun Shrimp Appetizer

Preparation time: 14 minutes **Cooking time:** 5 minutes **Servings:** 2

Ingredients:

- 20 tiger shrimp, peeled and deveined
- Salt and black pepper to the taste
- ½ teaspoon old bay seasoning
- 1 tablespoon olive oil
- ¼ teaspoon smoked paprika

Directions:

1. Toss the shrimp with the oil, salt, pepper, old berry seasoning and paprika.
2. Put the shrimp in your Air Fryer basket and cook at 390 degrees F for 5 minutes.
3. Arrange them on a platter and serve. Enjoy!

Nutrition: calories 163, fat 6, fiber 4, carbs 8, protein 14

80. Cheesy Party Wings

Preparation time: 13 minutes **Cooking time:** 12 minutes **Servings:** 6

Ingredients:

- 6-pound chicken wings halved
- Salt and black pepper
- ½ teaspoon Italian seasoning
- 2 tablespoons butter
- ½ cup parmesan cheese, grated

- A pinch of red pepper flakes, crushed
- 1 teaspoon garlic powder
- 1 egg

Directions:

1. Arrange chicken wings in your Air Fryer's basket, cook at 390 degrees F and cook for 9 minutes.
2. Meanwhile, mix butter with cheese, egg, salt, pepper, pepper flakes, garlic powder and Italian seasoning in your blender and blend well.
3. Take chicken wings out, pour cheese sauce over them, toss to coat well and cook in your Air Fryer's basket at 390 degrees F for 3 minutes.
4. Serve them as an appetizer. Enjoy!

Nutrition: calories 204, fat 8, fiber 1, carbs 18, protein 14

81. Cheesy Zucchini Snack

Preparation time: 14 minutes **Cooking time:** 8 minutes **Servings:** 4

Ingredients:

- 1 cup mozzarella, shredded
- ¼ cup tomato sauce
- 1 zucchini, sliced
- Salt and black pepper to the taste
- A pinch of cumin
- Cooking spray

Directions:

1. Arrange zucchini slices in your Air Fryer's basket. Spray them with cooking oil, spread tomato sauce all over them, season with salt, pepper and cumin, sprinkle mozzarella at the end and cook them at 320 degrees F for 8 minutes.
2. Arrange them on a platter and serve. Enjoy!

Nutrition: calories 150, fat 4, fiber 2, carbs 12, protein 4

82. Chicken Breast Rolls

Preparation time: 12 minutes **Cooking time:** 22 minutes **Servings:** 4

Ingredients:

- 2 cups baby spinach
- 4 chicken breasts, boneless and skinless
- 1 cup sun-dried tomatoes, chopped
- Salt and black pepper
- 1 and ½ tablespoons of Italian seasoning
- 4 mozzarella slices
- A drizzle of olive oil

Directions:

1. Flatten chicken breasts using a meat tenderizer, divide tomatoes, mozzarella and spinach, season with salt, pepper and Italian seasoning and roll and seal them.
2. Place them in your Air Fryer's basket, drizzle oil over them and cook at 375 degrees F for 17 minutes, flipping once.
3. Arrange chicken rolls on a platter. Enjoy!

Nutrition: calo 300, fat 1, fiber 4, carbs 7, protein 10

83. Chicken Dip

Preparation time: 10 minutes **Cooking time:** 25 minutes **Servings:** 10

Ingredients:

- 3 tablespoons butter, melted
- 1 cup yogurt
- 12 ounces cream cheese

- 2 cups chicken meat, cooked and shredded
- 2 teaspoons curry powder
- 4 scallions, chopped
- 6 ounces Monterey jack cheese, grated
- 1/3 cup raisins
- ¼ cup cilantro, chopped
- ½ cup almonds, sliced
- Salt and black pepper to the taste
- ½ cup chutney

Directions:

1. In a bowl, blend the cream cheese with the yogurt and whip it with your mixer.
2. Add curry powder, scallions, chicken meat, raisins, cheese, cilantro, salt and pepper and stir everything.
3. Spread this into a baking dish that fist your Air Fryer, sprinkle almonds on top, place in your Air Fryer, bake at 300 degrees for 25 minutes, divide into bowls, top with chutney and serve. Enjoy!

Nutrition: calories 240, fat 10, fiber 2, carbs 24, protein 12

84. Chicken Rolls

Preparation time: 2 hours and 10 minutes **Cooking time:** 10 minutes **Servings:** 12

Ingredients:

- 4 ounces blue cheese, crumbled
- 2 cups chicken, cooked and chopped
- Salt and black pepper to the taste
- 2 green onions, chopped
- 2 celery stalks, finely chopped
- ½ cup tomato sauce
- 12 egg roll wrappers
- Cooking spray

Directions:

1. Mix chicken meat with blue cheese, salt, pepper, green onions, celery and tomato

sauce, stir well and keep in the fridge for 2 hours.

2. Place egg wrappers on a working surface, divide chicken mix, and roll and seal edges.

3. Place rolls in your Air Fryer's basket, spray them with cooking oil and cook at 350 degrees F for 10 minutes, flipping them halfway. Enjoy!

Nutrition: calories 220, fat 7, fiber 2, carbs 14, protein 10

85. Chickpeas Snack

Preparation time: 12 minutes **Cooking time:** 10 minutes **Servings:** 4

Ingredients:

- 15 ounces canned chickpeas, drained
- ½ teaspoon cumin, ground
- 1 tablespoon olive oil
- 1 teaspoon smoked paprika
- Salt and black pepper to the taste

Directions:

1. Mix chickpeas with oil, cumin, paprika, salt and pepper, toss to coat, place them in your fryer's basket and cook at 390 degrees F for 10 minutes.

2. Divide into bowls and serve. Enjoy!

Nutrition: calories 140, fat 1, fiber 6, carbs 20, protein 6

86. Crispy Chicken Breast Sticks

Preparation time: 10 minutes **Cooking time:** 16 minutes **Servings:** 4

Ingredients:

- ¾ cup white flour
- 1 pound chicken breast, skinless, boneless and cut into medium sticks
- 1 teaspoon sweet paprika
- 1 cup panko breadcrumbs
- 1 egg, whisked

- Salt and black pepper to the taste
- ½ tablespoon olive oil
- Zest from 1 lemon, grated

Directions:

1. In a bowl, mix paprika with flour, salt, pepper and lemon zest and stir.

2. Put whisked egg in second bowl, the panko breadcrumbs in a third one.

3. Dredge chicken pieces in flour, egg and panko and place them in your lined Air Fryer's basket, drizzle the oil over them, cook at 400 degrees F for 8 minutes, flip and cook for 8 more minutes.

4. Arrange them on a platter and serve. Enjoy!

Nutrition: calories 254, fat 4, fiber 7, carbs 20, protein 22

87. Herbed Tomatoes Appetizer

Preparation time: 14 minutes **Cooking time:** 20 minutes **Servings:** 2

Ingredients:

- 2 tomatoes, halved
- Cooking spray
- Salt and black pepper to the taste
- 1 teaspoon parsley, dried
- 1 teaspoon basil, dried
- 1 teaspoon oregano, dried
- 1 teaspoon rosemary, dried

Directions:

1. Spray tomato halves with cooking oil and season with salt, pepper, parsley, basil, oregano, and rosemary over them.

2. Place them in your Air Fryer's basket and cook at 320 degrees F for 20 minutes.

3. Arrange them on a platter and serve. Enjoy!

Nutrition: calories 100, fat 1, fiber 1, carbs 4, protein 1

88. Honey Party Wings

Preparation time: 1 hour and 10 minutes **Cooking time:** 12 minutes **Servings:** 8

Ingredients:

- 16 chicken wings, halved
- 2 tablespoons soy sauce
- 2 tablespoons honey
- Salt and black pepper to the taste
- 2 tablespoons lime juice

Directions:

1. Mix chicken wings with soy sauce, honey, salt, pepper and lime juice, toss well and keep in the fridge for 1 hour.
2. Transfer chicken wings to your Air Fryer and cook them at 360 degrees F for 12 minutes, flipping them halfway.
3. Arrange them on a platter and serve. Enjoy!

Nutrition: calories 211, fat 4, fiber 7, carbs 14, protein 3

89. Jalapeno Balls

Preparation time: 10 minutes **Cooking time:** 4 minutes **Servings:** 3

Ingredients:

- 3 bacon slices, cooked and crumbled
- 3 ounces cream cheese
- ¼ teaspoon onion powder
- Salt and black pepper to the taste
- 1 jalapeno pepper, chopped
- ½ teaspoon parsley, dried
- ¼ teaspoon garlic powder

Directions:

1. Mix cream cheese with jalapeno pepper, onion and garlic powder, parsley, bacon salt and pepper and stir well.
2. Shape small balls out of this mix, place them in your Air Fryer's basket, cook at 350 degrees F for 4 minutes, arrange on a platter

and serve as an appetizer. Enjoy!

Nutrition: calories 172, fat 4, fiber 1, carbs 12, protein 5

90. Mexican Apple Snack

Preparation time: 12 minutes **Cooking time:** 5 minutes **Servings:** 4

Ingredients:

- 3 big apples, cored, peeled and cubed
- 2 teaspoons lemon juice
- ¼ cup pecans, chopped
- ½ cup dark chocolate chips
- ½ cup clean caramel sauce

Directions:

1. Mix apples with lemon juice, stir and transfer to a pan that fits your Air Fryer.
2. Add chocolate chips and pecans, drizzle the caramel sauce, toss, introduce in your Air Fryer and cook at 320 degrees F for 5 minutes.
3. Toss gently, divide into small bowls. Enjoy!

Nutrition: calories 200, fat 4, fiber 3, carbs 20, protein 3

91. Mushrooms Appetizer

Preparation time: 11 minutes **Cooking time:** 10 minutes **Servings:** 4

Ingredients:

- ¼ cup mayonnaise
- 1 teaspoon garlic powder
- 1 small yellow onion, chopped
- 24 ounces white mushroom caps
- Salt and black pepper to the taste
- 1 teaspoon curry powder
- 4 ounces cream cheese, soft
- ¼ cup sour cream
- ½ cup Mexican cheese, shredded
- 1 cup shrimp, cooked, peeled, deveined and chopped

Directions:

1. Mix mayo with garlic powder, onion, curry powder, cream cheese, sour cream, Mexican cheese, shrimp, salt and pepper to the taste and whisk well.
2. Stuff mushrooms with this mix, place them in your Air Fryer's basket and cook at 300 degrees F for 10 minutes.
3. Arrange on a platter and serve. Enjoy!

Nutrition: calories 200, fat 20, fiber 3, carbs 16, protein 14

92. Olives Balls

Preparation time: 10 minutes **Cooking time:** 4 minutes **Servings:** 6

Ingredients:

- 8 black olives, pitted and minced
- Salt and black pepper to the taste
- 2 tablespoons sun-dried tomato pesto
- 14 pepperoni slices, chopped
- 4 ounces of cream cheese
- 1 tablespoon basil, chopped

Directions:

1. Mix cream cheese with salt, pepper, basil, pepperoni, pesto and black olives, stir well and shape small balls out of this mix.
2. Place them in your Air Fryer's basket, cook at 350 degrees F for 4 minutes, arrange on a platter and serve as a snack. Enjoy!

Nutrition: calories 100, fat 1, fiber 0, carbs 8, protein 3

93. Pesto Crackers

Preparation time: 8 minutes **Cooking time:** 17 minutes **Servings:** 6

Ingredients:

- ½ teaspoon baking powder
- Salt and black pepper to the taste
- 1 and ¼ cups flour
- ¼ teaspoon basil, dried
- 1 garlic clove, minced
- 2 tablespoons basil pesto
- 3 tablespoons butter

Directions:

1. Mix salt, pepper, baking powder, flour, garlic, cayenne, basil, pesto and butter and stir until you obtain a dough.
2. Spread this dough on a lined baking sheet that fits your Air Fryer, introduce it in the fryer at 325 degrees F and bake for 17 minutes.
3. Leave aside to cool down, cut crackers and serve them as a snack. Enjoy!

Nutrition: calories 200, fat 20, fiber 1, carbs 4, protein 7

94. Pork Rolls

Preparation time: 9 minutes **Cooking time:** 40 minutes **Servings:** 4

Ingredients:

- 1 15 ounces pork fillet
- ½ teaspoon chili powder
- 1 teaspoon cinnamon powder
- 1 garlic clove, minced
- Salt and black pepper to the taste
- 2 tablespoons olive oil
- 1 and ½ teaspoon cumin, ground
- 1 red onion, chopped
- 3 tablespoons parsley, chopped

Directions:

1. Mix cinnamon with garlic, salt, pepper, chili powder, oil, onion, parsley and cumin and stir well.
2. Put pork fillet on a cutting board and flatten it using a meat tenderizer. And use a meat tenderizer to flatten it.
3. Spread onion mix on pork, roll tight, cut into medium rolls, place them in your preheated Air Fryer at 360 degrees F and cook them for 35 minutes.
4. Arrange them on a platter and serve. Enjoy!

Nutrition: calories 304, fat 12, fiber 1, carbs 15, protein 23

FISH & SEAFOOD

95. Asian Salmon

Preparation time: 1 hour **Cooking time:** 17 minutes **Servings:** 2

Ingredients:

- 2 medium salmon fillets
- 6 tablespoons light soy sauce
- 3 teaspoons mirin
- 1 teaspoon water
- 6 tablespoons honey

Directions:

1. Blend the soy sauce with the honey, water and mirin, whisk well, add the salmon, rub well and leave in the refrigerator for 1 hour.
2. Transfer the salmon to your air fryer and cook at 360° F for 15 minutes, turning them after 7 minutes.
3. Meanwhile, place the soy marinade in a skillet, heat over medium heat, whisk well, cook for 2 minutes, then remove the heat.
4. Spoon the salmon into the plates, drizzle with the marinade and serve. Enjoy!

Nutrition: cal. 302, fat 12, fiber 8, carbs 13, protein 24

96. Black Cod with Plum Sauce

Preparation time: 13 minutes **Cooking time:** 15 minutes **Servings:** 2

Ingredients:

- 1 egg white
- ½ cup red quinoa, pre-cooked
- 2 teaspoons of whole wheat flour
- 4 teaspoons lemon juice
- ½ teaspoon of smoked paprika
- 1 teaspoon of olive oil
- 2 medium black cod fillets, skinned and boneless
- 1 red plum, pitted and chopped
- 2 teaspoons raw honey
- ¼ teaspoon black peppercorns, crushed
- 2 teaspoons parsley
- ¼ cup water

Directions:

1. Mix 1 teaspoon of lemon juice with the egg white, flour and ¼ teaspoon of paprika and whip well. Put the quinoa in a bowl and add 1/3 of the egg white mixture.
2. Place the fish in the bowl with the remaining eggwhite mixture and toss to coat. Soak the fish in the quinoa mixture, cover thoroughly and set aside for 10 minutes.
3. Heat a skillet with 1 teaspoon of oil over medium heat; add pepper, honey and plum, stir, bring to a boil, and cook for 1 minute. Add the remaining lemon juice, paprika and water, mix thoroughly and simmer for 5 minutes.
4. Add the parsley, stir, remove the sauce from the heat, then set aside. Place the fish in your fryer and cook at 380°F for 10 minutes.
5. Arrange fish on plates, sprinkle with plum sauce and serve. Enjoy!

Nutrition: cal. 325, fat 14, fiber 22, carbs 27, prot 22

97. Buttered Shrimp Skewers

Preparation time: 11 minutes **Cooking time:** 6 minutes **Servings:** 2

Ingredients:

- 8 shrimps, peeled and deveined
- 4 garlic cloves, minced
- Salt and black pepper to the taste
- 8 green bell pepper slices
- 1 tablespoon rosemary, chopped
- 1 tablespoon butter, melted

Directions:

1. Blend the shrimp with the garlic, butter, salt, pepper, rosemary and pepper slices. Stir to coat and allow to stand for 10 minutes.
2. Place two shrimp and two pepper slices on a skewer and repeat with the remaining shrimp and pepper pieces.
3. Put them in the basket of your fryer and bake 360 degrees F for 6 minutes.
4. Divide among plates and serve. Enjoy!

Nutrition: calories 143, fat 1, fiber 12, carbs 15, protein 7

98. Chili Salmon

Preparation time: 14 minutes **Cooking time:** 15 minutes **Servings:** 12

Ingredients:

- 1 and ¼ cups coconut, shredded
- 1 pound salmon, cubed
- 1/3 cup flour
- A pinch of salt and black pepper
- 1 egg
- 2 tablespoons olive oil
- ¼ cup water
- 4 red chilies, chopped
- 3 garlic cloves, minced
- ¼ cup balsamic vinegar

- ½ cup honey

Directions:

1. Stir the flour with a pinch of salt. Mix the egg with the black pepper In a different bowl and beat with a whisk. Transfer the coconut to a third bowl.
2. Dip the salmon cubes in the flour, egg and coconut, put them in your Air Fryer basket, bake at 370 degrees F for 8 minutes, shaking mid-way and divide them into plates.
3. Heat a skillet with the water over medium-high heat, add the peppers, cloves, vinegar and honey, mix well.
4. Bring to a boil, simmer for a few minutes, baste with salmon and serve.
5. Enjoy!

Nutrition: cal. 222, fat 12, fiber 2, carbs 14, protein 13

99. Chine Cod

Preparation time: 16 minutes **Cooking time:** 10 minutes **Servings:** 2

Ingredients:

- 2 medium cod fillets, boneless
- 1 teaspoon peanuts, crushed
- 2 teaspoons garlic powder
- 1 tablespoon light soy sauce
- ½ teaspoon ginger, grated

Directions:

1. Put fish fillets in a heat-proof dish that suits your fryer, add garlic powder, soy sauce and ginger, mix well.
2. Turn on your Air Fryer and bake at 350 degrees Fahrenheit for 10 minutes.
3. Arrange fish on plates, sprinkle with peanuts and serve. Enjoy!

Nutrition: cal. 256, fat 10, fiber 11, carbs 14, protein 23

100. Coconut Tilapia

Preparation time: 17 minutes **Cooking time:** 10 minutes **Servings:** 4

Ingredients:

- 4 medium tilapia fillets
- Salt and black pepper to the taste
- ½ cup coconut milk
- 1 teaspoon ginger, grated
- ½ cup cilantro, chopped
- 2 garlic cloves, chopped
- ½ teaspoon garam masala
- Cooking spray
- ½ jalapeno, chopped

Directions:

1. Combine coconut milk with salt, pepper, coriander, ginger, garlic, jalapeno and garam masala in your food processor.
2. Coat fish with cooking spray and spread coconut mixture everywhere, rub well. Transfer to the basket of your frying machine and bake 10 minutes at 400°F.
3. Divide among plates and serve hot.
4. Enjoy!

Nutrition: calories 203, fat 5, fiber 6, carbs 25, protein 26

101. Cod and Vinaigrette

Preparation time: 16 minutes **Cooking time:** 15 minutes **Servings**: 4

Ingredients:

- 4 cod fillets, skinless and boneless
- 12 cherry tomatoes, halved
- 8 black olives, pitted and roughly chopped
- 2 tablespoons lemon juice
- Salt and black pepper to the taste
- 2 tablespoons olive oil
- Cooking spray
- 1 bunch of basil, chopped

Directions:

1. Add salt and pepper to the cod, place it in the basket of your air fryer and bake in the 360° F oven for 10 minutes, turning after 5 minutes. Meanwhile, heat saucepan with oil over medium heat.
2. Add tomatoes, olives and lemon juice and toss. Bring to a boil; add basil, salt and pepper, mix well and remove the heat.
3. Spoon the fish onto the plates and serve with the drizzled vinaigrette. Enjoy!

Nutrition: calories 303, fat 5, fiber 8, carbs 12, protein 8

102. Cod Fillets and Peas

Preparation time: 14 minutes **Cooking time:** 10 minutes **Servings**: 4

Ingredients:

- 4 cod fillets, boneless
- 2 tablespoons parsley, chopped
- 2 cups peas
- 4 tablespoons wine
- ½ teaspoon oregano, dried
- ½ teaspoon sweet paprika
- 2 garlic cloves, minced
- Salt and pepper to the taste

Directions:

1. Combine the garlic with the parsley, salt, pepper, oregano, paprika and wine in your robot. Rub the fish with half of this mix, place in your fryer and cook 10 minutes at 360 degrees F.

2. Meanwhile, put the peas in a saucepan, add the water to cover, add the salt, boil over medium- high heat, cook for 10 minutes, drain and divide between dishes.

3. Divide the fish among the plates, divide the remaining vinaigrette and serve. Enjoy!

Nutrition: cal. 262, fat 8, fiber 12, carbs 20, protein 23

103. Cod Fillets with Fennel and Grapes Salad

Preparation time: 13 minutes **Cooking time:** 15 minutes **Servings:** 2

Ingredients:

- 2 black cod fillets, boneless
- 1 tablespoon olive oil
- Salt and black pepper to the taste
- 1 fennel bulb, thinly sliced
- 1 cup grapes, halved
- ½ cup pecans

Directions:

1. Pour half of the oil over the fish fillets, add salt and pepper, rub well, place the fillets in your air fryer basket. Cook for 10 minutes at 400°F and transfer to a baking sheet.

2. In a bowl, combine the pecan nuts, grapes, fennel, remaining oil, salt and pepper. Add to a skillet which adapts to your air fryer and cook 5 minutes at 400 degrees F.

3. Divide the cod among the plates, add the fennel and grapes, toss to the side and serve.

Nutrition: calories 301, fat 4, fiber 2, carbs 32, protein 22

104. Cod Steaks with Plum Sauce

Preparation time: 14 minutes **Cooking time:** 20 minutes **Servings:** 2

Ingredients:

- 2 big cod steaks
- Salt and black pepper to the taste
- ½ teaspoon garlic powder

- ½ teaspoon ginger powder
- ¼ teaspoon turmeric powder
- 1 tablespoon plum sauce
- Cooking spray

Directions:

1. Add salt and pepper to the cod steaks, sprinkle with cooking oil, add the garlic powder, ginger and turmeric and rub well. Place the cod steaks in your fryer and cook 360 degrees F for 15 minutes, turning them around after 7 minutes.

2. Heat a skillet over medium heat, add the plum sauce, toss and cook for 2 minutes.

3. Divide cod steaks on plates, drizzle the plum sauce and serve. Enjoy!

Nutrition: calories 251, fat 7, fiber 1, carbs 14, protein 12

105. Cod with Pearl Onions

Preparation time: 11 minutes **Cooking time:** 15 minutes **Servings:** 2

Ingredients:

- 14 ounces pearl onions
- 2 medium cod fillets
- 1 tablespoon parsley, dried
- 1 teaspoon thyme, dried
- Black pepper to the taste
- 8 ounces mushrooms, sliced

Directions:

1. Place the fish on a heat-resistant plate suitable for your fryer, add the onions, parsley, mushrooms, thyme and black pepper and mix well.

2. Turn on your Air Fryer, bake at 350 degrees F, and bake for 15 minutes.

3. Divide everything among plates and serve. Enjoy!

Nutrition: calories 271, fat 14, fiber 8, carbs 14, protein 22

108. Flavored Jamaican Salmon

Preparation time: 16 minutes **Cooking time:** 10 minutes **Servings:** 4

Ingredients:

- 2 teaspoons of sriracha sauce
- 4 teaspoons sugar
- 3 scallions, minced
- Salt and black pepper
- 2 teaspoons of olive oil
- 4 teaspoons of apple cider vinegar
- 3 teaspoons avocado oil
- 4 medium salmon fillets, deboned
- 4 cups of baby arugula
- 2 cups cabbage, grated
- 1 and ½ teaspoon Jamaican jerk seasoning
- ¼ cup pepitas, toasted
- 2 cups radish, julienned

Directions:

1. Mix the sriracha with the sugar, whisk and transfer two teaspoons in another bowl. Stir 2 teaspoons of sriracha with avocado and olive oil, the vinegar, salt and pepper, whisk.
2. Sprinkle the jerky seasoning onto the salmon, rub with the sriracha and sugar, season with salt and pepper. Transfer to your fryer and bake in 360 degrees F for 10 minutes, turning once.
3. Blend radishes with cabbage, arugula, salt, pepper, sriracha and vinegar; mix well.
4. Spoon salmon and radish mixture onto plates, sprinkle with pepitas and green onions and serve. Enjoy!

Nutrition: calories 292, fat 6, fiber 12, carbs 17, protein 8

106. Creamy Salmon

Preparation time: 10 minutes   **Cooking time:** 10 minutes **Servings:** 4

Ingredients:

- 4 salmon fillets, boneless
- 1 tablespoon olive oil
- Salt and black pepper to the taste
- 1/3 cup cheddar cheese, grated
- 1 and ½ teaspoon mustard
- ½ cup coconut cream

Directions:

1. Add salt and pepper to the salmon, pour the oil and rub thoroughly. Blend the coconut cream with the cheddar, mustard, salt and pepper.
2. Transfer the salmon to a skillet that suits your fryer; add the mixture to the coconut cream, place in your fryer. Bake on 320° F for 10 minutes.
3. Divide among plates and serve. Enjoy!

Nutrition: cal. 203, fat 6, fiber 14, carbs 17, protei 20

107. Flavored Air Fried Salmon

Preparation time: 1- h o u r **Cooking time:** 9 minutes Servings: 2

Ingredients:

- 2 salmon fillets
- 2 tablespoons lemon juice
- Salt and black pepper
- ½ teaspoon of garlic powder
- 1/3 cup of water
- 1/3 cup of soy sauce
- 3 scallions, minced
- 1/3 cup of brown sugar
- 2 tablespoons of olive oil

Directions:

1. Blend the sugar with the water, soy sauce, garlic powder, salt, pepper, oil and lemon juice. Stir to coat and place in the refrigerator for 1 hour.
2. Transfer the salmon fillets to the basket and cook 8 minutes 360°F, turning mid-way.
3. Divide salmon on plates, sprinkle scallions on top and serve right away.

4. Enjoy!

Nutrition: calori 300, fat 12, fiber 10, carbs 23, protein 20

109. Mustard Salmon

Preparation time: 12 minutes **Cooking time:** 10 minutes **Servings**: 1

Ingredients:

- 1 big salmon fillet, boneless
- Salt and black pepper to the taste
- 2 tablespoons mustard
- 1 tablespoon coconut oil
- 1 tablespoon maple extract

Directions:

1. Mix maple extract with mustard, whisk well, season salmon with salt and pepper and brush salmon with this mix.
2. Spray some cooking spray over the fish, place in your Air Fryer and cook 10 minutes at 370 degrees F, flipping halfway.
3. Serve with a tasty side salad.
4. Enjoy!

110. Hawaiian Salmon

Preparation time: 17 minutes **Cooking time:** 10 minutes **Servings:** 2

Ingredients:

- 20 ounces of canned pineapple pieces and juice
- ½ teaspoon ginger, grated
- 2 teaspoons garlic powder
- 1 teaspoon onion powder
- 1 tablespoon balsamic vinegar
- 2 medium salmon fillets, boneless
- Salt and black pepper to the taste

Directions:

1. Sprinkle the salmon with the garlic powder, onion powder, salt and black pepper. Transfer to a heat-proof dish that adapts to your fryer, add the ginger and pineapple pieces and discard gently.
2. Drizzle the vinegar, put in your Air Fryer and cook for 10 minutes at 350 degrees F.
3. Divide everything on plates and serve. Enjoy!

Nutrition: calories 200, fat 8, fiber 12, crbs 17, protein 20

111. Oriental Fish

Preparation time: 14 minutes **Cooking time:** 12 minutes **Servings:** 4

Ingredients:

- 2 pounds red snapper fillets, boneless
- Salt and black pepper to the taste
- 3 garlic cloves, minced
- 1 yellow onion, chopped
- 1 tablespoon tamarind paste
- 1 tablespoon oriental sesame oil
- 1 tablespoon ginger, grated
- 2 tablespoons water
- ½ teaspoon cumin, ground
- 1 tablespoon lemon juice
- 3 tablespoons mint, chopped

Directions:

1. Using a food processor, combine the garlic with the onion, salt and pepper, tamarind paste, the sesame oil, ginger, water and cumin. Mix well and scrub the fish with this mixture.
2. Put the fish in your preheated fryer at 320 degrees F and bake for 12 minutes, turning the fish halfway.
3. Spoon the fish onto the plates, add the lemon juice, sprinkle with mint and serve immediately. Enjoy!

Nutrition: calories 242, fat 8, fiber 16, carbs 17, protein 12

112. Roasted Cod and Prosciutto

Preparation time: 12 minutes **Cooking time:** 10 minutes **Servings:** 4

Ingredients:

- 1 tablespoon parsley, chopped
- 4 medium cod filets
- ¼ cup butter, melted
- 2 garlic cloves, minced
- 2 tablespoons lemon juice
- 3 tablespoons prosciutto, chopped
- 1 teaspoon Dijon mustard
- 1 shallot, chopped
- Salt and black pepper

Directions:

1. Mix the mustard with the butter, garlic, parsley, shallot, lime juice, prosciutto, salt and pepper and beat well.
2. Season the fish with salt and pepper, spread the prosciutto mixture all over, place in the deep fryer and bake at 390 degrees F for 10 minutes.
3. Divide among plates and serve.
4. Enjoy!

Nutrition: calories 204, fat 4, fiber 7, carbs 12, protein 6

113. Salmon and Avocado Salsa

Preparation time: 35 minutes **Cooking time:** 10 minutes **Servings:** 4

Ingredients:

- 4 salmon fillets
- 1 tablespoon olive oil
- Salt and black pepper to the taste
- 1 teaspoon cumin, ground
- 1 teaspoon sweet paprika
- ½ teaspoon chili powder
- 1 teaspoon garlic powder

For the salsa:

- 1 small red onion, chopped
- 1 avocado, pitted, peeled and chopped
- 2 tablespoons cilantro, chopped
- Juice from 2 limes
- Salt and black pepper to the taste

Directions:

1. Mix salt, pepper, chili powder, onion powder, paprika and cumin, stir, rub salmon with this mix, drizzle the oil, rub again, transfer to your Air Fryer and bake at 350 degrees F for 5 minutes on each side.
2. Meanwhile, in a bowl, mix avocado with red onion, salt, pepper, cilantro and lime juice and stir.
3. Divide fillets on plates, top with avocado salsa and serve. Enjoy!

Nutrition: cal. 300, fat 14, fiber 4, carbs 18, protei 16

114. Salmon and Avocado Sauce

Preparation time: 16 minutes **Cooking time:** 10 minutes **Servings:** 4

Ingredients:

- 1 avocado, pitted, peeled and chopped
- 4 salmon fillets, boneless
- ¼ cup cilantro, chopped
- 1/3 cup coconut milk

- 1 tablespoon lime juice
- 1 tablespoon lime zest, grated
- 1 teaspoon onion powder
- 1 teaspoon garlic powder
- Salt and black pepper to the taste

Directions:

1. Sprinkle the salmon fillets with salt, black pepper and lime zest. Put in your fryer, and bake 9 minutes at 350 degrees F, turning once and dividing between plates.
2. Blend the avocado with the cilantro, garlic and onion powder, lime juice, salt and pepper and coconut milk.
3. Toss to combine, drizzle with salmon and serve immediately.

4. Enjoy!

Nutrition: calories 261, fat 7, fiber 20, carbs 28, protein 18

115. Salmon and Blackberry Glaze

Preparation time: 12 minutes **Cooking time:** 33 minutes **Servings:** 4

Ingredients:

- 1 cup water
- 1-inch ginger piece, grated
- Juice from ½ lemon
- 12 ounces blackberries
- 1 tablespoon olive oil
- ¼ cup sugar
- 4 medium salmon fillets, skinless
- Salt and black pepper to the taste

Directions:

1. Heat a saucepan with the water over medium-high heat, add the ginger, lemon juice and blackberries, toss, bring to a boil. Bake for 4-5 minutes, remove the heat, sift in a bowl, return to the pan and mix with the sugar.

2. Stir the mixture until simmered over medium-

low heat and cook for 20 minutes. Let the blackberry sauce cool down, brush with salmon, season with salt and pepper, drizzle with olive oil and rub the fish well.

3. Place the fish in your pre-heated 350°F air fryer and cook for 10 minutes, turning the fish fillets once.

4. Arrange in plates, drizzle with remaining blackberry sauce and serve. Enjoy!

Nutrition: calories 313, fat 4, fiber 9, carbs 19, protein 14

116. Trout and Butter Sauce

Preparation time: 10 minutes **Cooking time:** 10 minutes **Servings:** 4

Ingredients:

- 4 trout fillets, boneless
- Salt and black pepper to the taste
- 3 teaspoons lemon zest, grated
- 3 tablespoons chives, chopped
- 6 tablespoons butter
- 2 tablespoons olive oil
- 2 teaspoons lemon juice

Directions:

1. Season trout with salt and pepper, drizzle the olive oil, rub, transfer to your Air Fryer and cook at 360 degrees F for 10 minutes, flipping once.

2. Meanwhile, heat a pan with the butter over medium heat; add salt, pepper, chives, lemon juice and zest, whisk well, cook for 1-2 minutes and take off the heat.

3. Divide fish fillets on plates, drizzle butter sauce all over and serve. Enjoy!

Nutrition: cal. 300, fat 12, fiber 9, carbs 27, protein 24

POULTRY

117. Chicken and Black Olives Sauce

Preparation time: 12 minutes **Cooking time:** 8 minutes

Servings: 2

Ingredients:

- 1 chicken breast cut into 4 pieces
- 2 tablespoons olive oil
- 3 garlic cloves, minced

For the sauce:

- 1 cup black olives, pitted
- Salt and black pepper to the taste
- 2 tablespoons olive oil
- ¼ cup parsley, chopped
- 1 tablespoon lemon juice

Directions:

1. In your food processor, mix the olives with the salt, pepper, 2 tbsp olive oil, lemon juice and parsley, mix well and transfer to a bowl.
2. Add salt and pepper to the the chicken, rub with oil and garlic, put in your pre-warmed air fryer and bake at 370 degrees F for 8 minutes.
3. Spread the chicken over the plates, drizzle with the olive sauce and serve. Enjoy!

Nutrition: cal. 271, fat 12, fiber 12, carbs 23, prot 22

118. Chicken and Capers

Preparation time: 14 minutes **Cooking time:** 20 minutes **Servings:** 2

Ingredients:

- 4 chicken thighs
- 3 tablespoons capers
- 4 garlic cloves, minced
- 3 tablespoons butter, melted
- Salt and black pepper to the taste

- ½ cup chicken stock
- 1 lemon, sliced
- 4 green onions, chopped

Directions:

1. Brush the chicken with butter, sprinkle with salt and pepper to taste, and place in an oven-proof dish that suits your fryer. Add capers, garlic, chicken broth and lemon slices and stir to coat.
2. Transfer to your fryer and cook for 20 minutes at 370 degrees F, stirring halfway.
3. Sprinkle with green onions, place on plates and serve. Enjoy!

Nutrition: calories 200, fat 9, fiber 10, carbs 17, protein 7

119. Chicken and Cauliflower Rice

Preparation time: 16 minutes **Cooking time:** 20 minutes **Servings:** 6

Ingredients:

- 3 bacon slices, chopped
- 3 carrots, chopped
- 3 pounds chicken thighs, boneless and skinless
- 2 bay leaves
- ¼ cup red wine vinegar
- 4 garlic cloves, minced
- Salt and black pepper to the taste

- 4 tablespoons olive oil
- 1 tablespoon garlic powder
- 1 tablespoon Italian seasoning
- 24 ounces cauliflower rice
- 1 teaspoon turmeric powder
- 1 cup beef stock

Directions:

1. Heat a frying pan suitable for your air fryer over medium-high heat; add the bacon, carrots, onion and garlic, stir and bake for 8 minutes.
2. Stir in chicken, oil, vinegar, turmeric, garlic powder, Italian pepper and bay leaves. Transfer to a deep fryer and cook for 12 minutes at 360° F.
3. Add rice and cauliflower broth, stir, bake for 6 minutes, divide among plates. Enjoy!

Nutrition: calories 342, fat 12, fiber 12, carbs 16, protein 8

120. Chicken and Chestnuts

Preparation time: 13 minutes **Cooking time:** 12 minutes **Servings:** 2

Ingredients:

- ½ pound chicken pieces
- 1 small yellow onion, chopped
- 2 teaspoons garlic, minced
- A pinch of ginger, grated
- A bit of allspice, ground
- 4 tablespoons water chestnuts
- 2 tablespoons soy sauce
- 2 tablespoons chicken stock
- 2 tablespoons balsamic vinegar
- 2 tortillas for serving

Directions:

1. In a skillet, combine the chicken meat with the onion, garlic, ginger, allspice, chestnuts, soy sauce, broth and vinegar. Transfer to your air fryer and bake at 360° F for 12 minutes.
2. Divide everything on plates and serve.

3. Enjoy!

Nutrition: calories 301, fat 12, fiber 7, crbs 24, protein 12

121. Chicken and Garlic Sauce

Preparation time: 14 minutes **Cooking time:** 20 minutes **Servings:** 4

Ingredients:

- 1 tablespoon butter, melted
- 4 chicken breasts, skin-on and bone-in
- 1 tablespoon olive oil
- Salt and black pepper to the taste
- 40 garlic cloves, peeled and chopped
- 2 thyme sprigs
- ¼ cup chicken stock
- 2 tablespoons parsley, chopped
- ¼ cup dry white wine

Directions:

1. Salt and pepper the chicken breast, rub with the oil, place in your deep fryer, bake 4 minutes at 360°F on each side. Transfer to a heat proof dish fitting your fryer.
2. Add the melted butter, garlic, thyme, soup, wine and parsley. Cook on 350°F for 15 minutes.
3. Divide everything among plates and serve.

Nutrition: calories 227, fat 9, fiber 13, crbs 22, protein 12

122. Chicken and Green Onions Sauce

Preparation time: 13 minutes **Cooking time:** 16 minutes **Servings:** 4

Ingredients:

- 10 green onions, roughly chopped
- 1-inch piece of ginger root, chopped
- 4 garlic cloves, minced
- 2 tablespoons fish sauce
- 3 tablespoons soy sauce
- 1 teaspoon Chinese five-spice

- 10 chicken drumsticks
- 1 cup coconut milk
- Salt and black pepper to the taste
- 1 teaspoon butter, melted
- ¼ cup cilantro, chopped
- 1 tablespoon lime juice

Directions:

1. Blend the green onions with the ginger, garlic, soy sauce, fish sauce, five spices, salt, pepper, butter and coconut milk in your food processor.
2. Mix chicken with green onions in a bowl, mix well, transfer everything to a pan that fits your deep fryer. Bake at 370°F for 16 minutes, shaking the fryer once.
3. Arrange in the plates, sprinkle with cilantro, drizzle with lime juice and serve with a side salad. Enjoy!

Nutrition: calories 322, fat 12, fiber 12, carbs 22, protein 20

123. Chicken and Lentils Casserole

Preparation time: 12 minutes **Cooking time:** 1-hour **Servings:** 8

Ingredients:

- 1 and ½ cups green lentils
- 3 cups chicken stock
- 2-pound chicken breasts, skinless, boneless and chopped
- Salt and cayenne pepper to the taste
- 3 teaspoons cumin, ground
- Cooking spray
- 5 garlic cloves, minced
- 1 yellow onion, chopped
- 2 red bell peppers, chopped
- 14 ounces canned tomatoes, chopped
- 2 cups corn
- 2 cups Cheddar cheese, shredded
- 2 tablespoons jalapeno pepper, chopped
- 1 tablespoon garlic powder
- 1 cup cilantro, chopped

Directions:

1. Add the broth to a saucepan, season with salt, add the lentils and stir. Bring to a boil over moderate heat, cover and simmer for 35 minutes.
2. In the meantime, spray the chicken pieces with a little cooking spray, add salt, cayenne pepper and 1 teaspoon of cumin. Put them in your Air Fryer basket and cook them for 6 minutes at 370°F, going back halfway.
3. Transfer chicken to a heat-resistant pan suitable for your deep fryer; add peppers, garlic, tomatoes, onion, salt, cayenne pepper and 1 teaspoon of cumin. Strain the lentils and add to the chicken mixture.
4. Add the jalapeño pepper, garlic powder, remaining cumin, corn, half the cheese and half the cilantro. Spoon into the air fryer and bake at 320°F for 25 minutes.
5. Sprinkle with remaining cheese and cilantro, top with chicken casserole and serve. Enjoy!

Nutrition: cal. 345, fat 11, fiber 12, carbs 22, prot 33

124. Chicken and Parsley Sauce

Preparation time: 28 minutes **Cooking time:** 25 minutes **Servings:** 6

Ingredients:

1. 1 cup parsley, chopped
2. 1 teaspoon oregano, dried
3. ½ cup olive oil
4. ¼ cup red wine
5. 4 garlic cloves

6. A pinch of salt
7. A drizzle of maple syrup
8. 12 chicken thighs

Directions:

1. Blend parsley with oregano, garlic, salt, oil, wine and maple syrup in your food processor. Combine the chicken and parsley sauce, mix well and store in the refrigerator for 30 minutes.
2. Drain the chicken, transfer it to your fryer's basket and cook for 25 minutes at 380°F, flipping it once.
3. Place the chicken on the plates, sprinkle with parsley sauce and serve. Enjoy!

Nutrition: cal. 355, fat 10, fiber 12, carbs 22, prot 17

125. Chicken and Peaches

Preparation time: 14 minutes **Cooking time:** 30 minutes **Servings:** 6

Ingredients:

- 1 whole chicken, cut into medium chunks
- ¾ cup of water
- 1/3 cup of honey
- Salt and black pepper
- ¼ cup of olive oil
- 4 peaches, cut in half

Directions:

1. Pour the water into a pan, boil over medium heat, add the honey, whisk well and set aside. Rub the chicken pieces with the oil, salt and pepper, put them in the basket of your deep fryer.
2. Bake at 350°F for 10 minutes. Brush the chicken with a portion of the honey mixture, cook for 6 more minutes and turn over again. Brush again with the honey mixture and bake for another 7 minutes.
3. Spoon the chicken pieces onto the plates and keep warm. Brush the peaches with the rest of the honey marinade, place them in your deep

fryer and cook them for 3 minutes.
4. Place on the plates next to the chicken pieces. Enjoy!

Nutrition: calories 432, fat 14, fiber 3, carbs 15, protein 20

126. Chicken and Radish

Preparation time: 13 minutes **Cooking time:** 30 minutes **Servings:** 4

Ingredients:

- 4 chicken things, bone-in
- Salt and black pepper to the taste
- 1 tablespoon olive oil
- 1 cup chicken stock
- 6 radishes, halved
- 1 teaspoon sugar
- 3 carrots, cut into thin sticks
- 2 tablespoons chives, chopped

Directions:

1. Heat a skillet that adapts to your fryer Air over medium heat, add the stock, carrots, sugar and radishes, stir gently. Reduce heat to medium, cover part of pan and let simmer for 20 minutes.
2. Rub the chicken with the olive oil, add salt and pepper, place in the fryer. Cook at 350°F for 4 minutes.
3. Add the chicken to the radish mixture, toss, place everything in your fryer, bake for 4 minutes more, divide among plates. Enjoy!

Nutrition: calories 237, fat 10, fiber 4, crbs 19, protein 29

127. Chicken and Coconut Sauce

Preparation time: 14 minutes **Cooking time:** 12 minutes **Servings:** 6

Ingredients:

- 1 tablespoon olive oil
- 3 and ½ pounds of chicken breasts

- 1 cup chicken stock
- 1 and ¼ cups yellow onion, chopped
- 1 tablespoon lime juice
- ¼ cup coconut milk
- 2 teaspoons sweet paprika
- 1 teaspoon red pepper flakes
- 2 tablespoons green onions, chopped
- Salt and black pepper to the taste

Directions:

1. Heat a frying pan that suits your air fryer with the oil over medium-high heat, add the onions, stir and cook for 4 minutes.
2. Add the broth, salt and pepper, coconut milk, pepper flakes, paprika and lime juice, and toss to combine.
3. Add chicken to skillet, add salt and pepper and mix well. Introduce into your air fryer and bake at 360°F for 12 minutes.
4. Divide chicken and sauce among plates.

Nutrition: calories 320, fat 13, fiber 13, carbs 32, protein 23

128. Chinese Stuffed Chicken

Preparation time: 17 minutes **Cooking time:** 35 minutes **Servings:** 8

Ingredients:

- 1 whole chicken
- 10 wolfberries
- 2 red chilies, chopped
- 4 ginger slices
- 1 yam, cubed
- 1 teaspoon soy sauce
- Salt and white pepper to the taste
- 3 teaspoons sesame oil

Directions:

1. Add salt and pepper to the chicken, rub with the soy sauce and the sesame oil and stuff with wolfberries, yam cubes, chilies and ginger.
2. Put in your fryer, bake for 20 minutes at 400°F, then 360°F for 15 minutes.

3. Carve chicken, divide among plates and serve. Enjoy!

Nutrition: cal. 320, fat 12, fiber 17, carbs 22, prot 12

129. Cider-Glazed Chicken

Preparation time: 11 minutes **Cooking time:** 14 minutes **Servings:** 4

Ingredients:

- 1 sweet potato, cubed
- 2 apples, cored and sliced
- 1 tablespoon olive oil
- 1 tablespoon rosemary, chopped
- Salt and black pepper to the taste
- 6 chicken thighs, bone-in and skin on
- 2/3 cup apple cider
- 1 tablespoon mustard
- 2 tablespoons honey
- 1 tablespoon butter

Directions:

1. Heat a frying pan suitable for your air fryer with half the oil over medium-high heat; add the cider, honey, butter and mustard, whisking thoroughly.
2. Cook, remove heat, add chicken and stir to combine. In a bowl, blend the potato cubes with the rosemary, apples, salt, pepper and remaining oil.
3. Toss to combine and add to the chicken mixture. Put the pans into your air fryer and cook for 14 minutes at 390°F.
4. Divide everything on plates and serve. Enjoy!

Nutrition: cal. 241, fat 7, fiber 12, carbs 28, protein 22

130. Creamy Chicken, Rice and Peas

Preparation time: 17 minutes **Cooking time:** 30 minutes **Servings:** 4

Ingredients:

- 1 pound chicken breasts, skinless, boneless and cut into quarters

- 1 cup white rice, already cooked
- Salt and black pepper to the taste
- 1 tablespoon olive oil
- 3 garlic cloves, minced
- 1 yellow onion, chopped
- ½ cup white wine
- ¼ cup heavy cream
- 1 cup chicken stock
- ¼ cup parsley, chopped
- 2 cups peas, frozen
- 1 and ½ cups parmesan, grated

Directions:

1. Add salt and pepper to the chicken breasts, pour half the oil over them, rub well and place in your Air Fryer basket. Bake at 360° F for 6 minutes.
2. Heat a saucepan with the remaining oil on medium-high heat. Add garlic, onion, wine, broth, salt, pepper and heavy cream.
3. Transfer the chicken breasts to a heat-resistant dish suitable for your air fryer. Add the peas, rice and cream on them and sprinkle the Parmesan and parsley everywhere.
4. Transfer to the fryer and cook for 10 minutes at 420°F.
5. Divide among plates and serve hot. Enjoy!

Nutrition: calorie 313, fat 12, fiber 14, crbs 27, protein 44

131. Creamy Coconut Chicken

Preparation time: 2 hours **Cooking time:** 25 minutes **Servings:** 4

Ingredients:

- 4 big chicken legs
- 5 teaspoons turmeric powder
- 2 tablespoons ginger, grated
- Salt and black pepper to the taste
- 4 tablespoons coconut cream

Directions:

1. Mix the cream with the turmeric, ginger, salt

and pepper, whip, add the chicken pieces, mix well and let rest for 2 hours.
2. Transfer chicken to your preheated air fryer and cook for 25 minutes at 370°F.
3. Spoon into dishes and serve with a salad.

Nutrition: cal. 300, fat 4, fiber 12, carbs 22, prot 20

132. Duck and Cherries

Preparation time: 14 minutes **Cooking time:** 20 minutes **Servings:** 4

Ingredients:

- ½ cup sugar and ¼ cup honey
- 1/3 cup balsamic vinegar
- 1 teaspoon garlic, minced
- 1 tablespoon ginger, grated
- 1 teaspoon cumin, ground
- ½ teaspoon clove, ground
- ½ teaspoon cinnamon powder
- 4 sage leaves, chopped
- 1 jalapeno, chopped
- 2 cups rhubarb, sliced
- ½ cup yellow onion, chopped
- 2 cups cherries, pitted
- 4 duck breasts, deboned, skin on and scored
- Salt and black pepper

Directions:

1. Add salt and pepper to the duck breast, put in the Air Fryer and bake for 5 minutes at 350°F on each side. Meanwhile, heat a skillet to medium.
2. Add the sugar, honey, cinnamon, sage, vinegar, garlic, ginger, cumin, clove, jalapeno, rhubarb, and onion cherries. Add duck

breasts, toss well, divide everything between plates and serve. Enjoy!

Nutrition: cal. 456, fat 13, fiber 4, carbs 64, protei 31

133. Duck and Plum Sauce

Preparation time: 10 minutes **Cooking time:** 32 minutes **Servings:** 2

Ingredients:

- 2 duck breasts
- 1 tablespoon butter, melted
- 1-star anise
- 1 tablespoon olive oil
- 1 shallot, chopped
- 9 ounces red plumps, stoned, cut into small wedges
- 2 tablespoons sugar
- 2 tablespoons red wine
- 1 cup beef stock

Directions:

1. Heat a saucepan with the olive oil on medium heat, add the shallot, mix and bake for 5 minutes. Add the sugar and plums, stir and cook until the sugar melts.
2. Add the stock and wine, stir, bake for 15 minutes, remove the heat and keep warm for now. Grate the magrets, season with salt and pepper and rub with the melted butter.
3. Transfer to a heat-proof pan suitable for your fryer, add star anise and plum sauce, place in your fryer and cook at 360°F for 12 minutes.
4. Split everything into plates. Enjoy!

Nutrition: cal. 400, fat 25, fiber 12, carbs 29, prot 44

134. Duck and Tea Sauce

Preparation time: 9 minutes **Cooking time:** 20 minutes Servings: 4

Ingredients:

- 2 duck breast halves, boneless
- 2 and ¼ cup chicken stock

- ¾ cup shallot, chopped
- 1 and ½ cup orange juice
- Salt and black pepper to the taste
- 3 teaspoons earl gray tea leaves
- 3 tablespoons butter, melted
- 1 tablespoon honey

Directions:

1. Add salt and pepper to the duck breast halves, place them in the preheated air fryer and bake at 360°F for 10 minutes.
2. In the meantime, heat a frying pan with the butter over medium heat, add the shallot, stir and cook for 2-3 minutes. Stir in the broth and cook for another minute.
3. Add the orange juice, tea leaves and honey, stir and cook for 2-3 minutes and strain into a bowl.
4. Spoon the duck into the plates, drizzle with the tea sauce and serve. Enjoy!

Nutrition: cal. 228, fat 11, fiber 2, carbs 20, protei 12

135. Greek Chicken

Preparation time: 16 minutes **Cooking time:** 15 minutes **Servings:** 4

Ingredients:

- 2 tablespoons olive oil
- Juice from 1 lemon
- 1 teaspoon oregano, dried
- 3 garlic cloves, minced
- 1 pound chicken thighs
- Salt and black pepper to the taste
- ½ pound asparagus, trimmed
- 1 zucchini, roughly chopped
- 1 lemon sliced

Directions:

1. In a heatproof dish that fits your Air Fryer, mix chicken pieces with oil, lemon juice, oregano, garlic, salt and pepper, asparagus, zucchini and lemon slices, toss, introduce in preheated Air Fryer and cook for 15 minutes

at 380 degrees F.

2. Divide everything among plates. Enjoy!

Nutrition: cal. 300, fat 8, fiber 12, carbs 20, protei 18

136. Herbed Chicken

Preparation time: 32 minutes **Cooking time:** 40 minutes **Servings:** 4

Ingredients:

- 1 whole chicken
- Salt and black pepper to the taste
- 1 teaspoon garlic powder
- 1 teaspoon onion powder
- ½ teaspoon thyme, dried
- 1 teaspoon rosemary, dried
- 1 tablespoon lemon juice
- 2 tablespoons olive oil

Directions:

1. Salt and pepper the chicken, rub with the thyme, rosemary, garlic powder and onion powder. Rub in the lemon juice and olive oil and set aside for 30 minutes.
2. Place the chicken in your air fryer and bake at 360 degrees F for 20 minutes per side.
3. Let the chicken chill, cut and serve. Enjoy!

Nutrition: calories 390, fat 10, fiber 5, carbs 22, protein 20

137. Honey Duck Breasts

Preparation time: 13 minutes **Cooking time:** 22 minutes **Servings:** 2

Ingredients:

- 1 smoked duck breast, halved
- 1 teaspoon honey
- 1 teaspoon tomato paste
- 1 tablespoon mustard
- ½ teaspoon apple vinegar

Directions:

1. Mix the honey with the tomato paste, mustard

and vinegar, whisk well, add the slices of duck breast and mix well. Transfer to your air fryer and bake at 370°F for 15 minutes.

2. Remove the duck breast from the fryer, add to the honey mixture, stir again, return to the Air fryer and bake at 370°F for 6 minutes.
3. Spoon into the dishes and serve with a salad. Enjoy!

Nutrition: cal. 274, fat 11, fiber 13, carbs 22, prot 13

138. Italian Chicken

Preparation time: 12 minutes **Cooking time:** 16 minutes **Servings:** 4

Ingredients:

- 5 chicken thighs
- 1 tablespoon olive oil
- 2 garlic cloves, minced
- 1 tablespoon thyme, chopped
- ½ cup heavy cream
- ¾ cup chicken stock
- 1 teaspoon red pepper flakes, crushed
- ¼ cup parmesan, grated
- ½ cup sun-dried tomatoes
- 2 tablespoons basil, chopped
- Salt and black pepper

Directions:

1. Season the chicken with salt and pepper, rub with half the oil, place in your air fryer preheated to 350°F and bake for 4 minutes. In the meantime, heat one pan with the remaining oil over medium- high heat.
2. Add thyme, garlic, pepper flakes, sun-dried tomatoes, heavy cream, stock, Parmesan, salt and pepper, stir and bring to a boil. Take out of the heat and transfer to a dish that matches your fryer.
3. Add the chicken legs to the top, insert into your fryer and bake at 320°F for 12 minutes.
4. Divide between plates and serve with the basil sprinkled over top. Enjoy!

Nutrition: cal. 272, fat 9, fiber 12, carbs 37, prot 23

139. Quick Creamy Chicken Casserole

Preparation time: 13 minutes **Cooking time:** 12 minutes **Servings:** 4

Ingredients:

- 10 ounces spinach, chopped
- 4 tablespoons butter
- 3 tablespoons flour
- 1 and ½ cups milk
- ½ cup parmesan, grated
- ½ cup heavy cream
- Salt and black pepper to the taste
- 2 cups chicken breasts, skinless, boneless and cubed
- 1 cup breadcrumbs

Directions:

1. Heat a pan with the butter over medium heat, add flour and stir well.
2. Add milk, heavy cream and parmesan, stir well, cook for 1-2 minutes more and take off the heat.
3. In a pan that fits your Air Fryer, spread chicken and spinach. Add salt and pepper and toss.
4. Add cream mixture and spread, sprinkle breadcrumbs on top, introduce in your Air Fryer and cook at 350 for 12 minutes.
5. Divide chicken and spinach mix on plates and serve. Enjoy!

Nutrition: cal. 321, fat 9, fiber 12, carbs 22, protein 17

MEAT

140. Beef and Cabbage Mix

Preparation time: 13 minutes **Cooking time:** 40 minutes **Servings:** 6

Ingredients:

- 2 and ½ pounds beef brisket
- 1 cup of beef stock
- 2 bay leaves
- 3 garlic cloves, chopped
- 4 carrots, chopped
- 1 cabbage head, cut into medium wedges
- Salt and black pepper to the taste
- 3 turnips, cut into quarters

Directions:

1. Put the beef breast and stock in a large saucepan that adapts to your fryer and season the beef with salt and pepper. Stir in garlic, bay leaves, carrots, cabbage, potatoes and turnips.
2. Insert into the fryer and bake at 360°F for 40 minutes.
3. Divide among plates and serve.
4. Enjoy!

Nutrition: cal. 354, fat 16, fiber 7, carbs 20, protein 24

141. Beef and Green Onions Marinade

Preparation time: 14 minutes **Cooking time:** 20 minutes **Servings:** 4

Ingredients:

- 1 cup green onion, chopped
- 1 cup soy sauce
- ½ cup water
- ¼ cup brown sugar
- ¼ cup sesame seeds
- 5 garlic cloves, minced
- 1 teaspoon black pepper
- 1-pound lean beef

Directions:

1. Mix onion, soy sauce, water, sugar, garlic, sesame seeds and pepper and whisk. Add meat, toss and set aside for 10 minutes.
2. Drain the beef, transfer it to the preheated air fryer and bake at 390°F for 20 minutes.
3. Slice, place on plates and serve with a side salad. Enjoy!

Nutrition: calories 330, fat 8, fiber 12, carbs 26, protein 22

142. Beef Casserole

Preparation time: 35 minutes **Cooking time:** 35 minutes **Servings:** 12

Ingredients:

- 1 tablespoon olive oil
- 2 pounds beef, ground
- 2 cups eggplant, chopped
- Salt and black pepper to the taste
- 2 teaspoons mustard
- 2 teaspoons gluten-free Worcestershire sauce
- 28 ounces canned tomatoes, chopped

- 2 cups mozzarella, grated
- 16 ounces tomato sauce
- 2 tablespoons parsley, chopped
- 1 teaspoon oregano, dried

Directions:

1. Mix the eggplants with the salt, pepper and oil and coat thoroughly. Combine beef with salt, pepper, mustard, and Worcestershire sauce in another bowl.
2. Mix well and place on the bottom of a frying pan that suits your fryer. Add eggplant mix, tomatoes, tomato sauce, parsley, and oregano and sprinkle mozzarella at the end. Introduce in your Air Fryer and bake at 360°F for 35 minutes.
3. Divide among plates and serve hot. Enjoy!

Nutrition: ca. 203, fat 12, fiber 2, carbs 16, prote 15

143. Beef Curry

Preparation time: 14 minutes **Cooking time:** 45 minutes **Servings:** 4

Ingredients:

- 2 pounds beef steak, cubed
- 2 tablespoons olive oil
- 3 potatoes, cubed
- 1 tablespoon wine mustard
- 2 and ½ tablespoons of curry powder
- 2 yellow onions, chopped
- 2 garlic cloves, minced
- 10 ounces of canned coconut milk
- 2 tablespoons tomato sauce
- Salt and black pepper to the taste

Directions:

1. Heat a frying pan suitable for your air fryer with the oil at medium-high heat, add the onions and garlic, stir and bake for 4 minutes.
2. Add the potatoes and mustard, blend and cook for 1 minute. Stir in the beef, curry, salt, pepper, coconut milk and tomato sauce.
3. Transfer to your Air Fryer and bake at 360°F

for 40 minutes.
4. Arrange in bowls and serve. Enjoy!

Nutrition: cal. 435, fat 16, fiber 4, carbs 20, protei 27

144. Beef Fillets with Garlic Mayo

Preparation time: 10 minutes **Cooking time:** 40 minutes **Servings:** 8

Ingredients:

- 1 cup mayonnaise
- 1/3 cup sour cream
- 2 garlic cloves, minced
- 3 pounds beef fillet
- 2 tablespoons of chives, chopped
- 2 tablespoons mustard
- ¼ cup tarragon, chopped
- Salt and black pepper

Directions:

1. Season the beef with salt and pepper to the taste, put it in your Air Fryer, and cook at 370°F for 20 minutes. Place on a platter and set aside for a few minutes.
2. In a bowl, combine the garlic with the sour cream, chives, mayo, salt and pepper, whisk and set aside. Toss mustard and tarragon in another bowl and whisk.
3. Add the beef, stir, flip to your air fryer, and cook at 350°F for 20 minutes more.
4. Divide the beef between the plates. Enjoy!

Nutrition: calories 402, fat 12, fiber 2, carbs 27, protein 19

145. Beef Kabobs

Preparation time: 11 minutes **Cooking time:** 10 minutes **Servings:** 4

Ingredients:

- 2 red bell peppers, chopped
- 2 pounds sirloin steak, cut into medium pieces
- 1 red onion, chopped

- 1 zucchini, sliced
- Juice from 1 lime
- 2 tablespoons chili powder
- 2 tablespoons hot sauce
- ½ tablespoons cumin, ground
- ¼ cup olive oil
- ¼ cup salsa
- Salt and black pepper to the taste

Directions:

1. Mix salsa with lime juice, oil, hot sauce, chili powder, cumin, salt and black pepper and whisk well.
2. Divide meat, bell peppers, zucchini and onion on skewers and brush kabobs with the salsa mix you made earlier.
3. Put them in your preheated Air Fryer and cook them for 10 minutes at 370°F, flipping the kabobs halfway.
4. Divide between plates and serve with a side salad. Enjoy!

Nutrition: calories 170, fat 5, fiber 2, carbs 13, protein 16

146. Beef Medallions Mix

Preparation time: 2 hours **Cooking time:** 10 minutes **Servings:** 4

Ingredients:

- 2 teaspoons chili powder
- 1 cup tomatoes, crushed
- 4 beef medallions
- 2 teaspoons onion powder
- 2 tablespoons soy sauce
- Salt and black pepper to the taste
- 1 tablespoon hot pepper
- 2 tablespoons lime juice

Directions:

1. In a bowl, mix tomatoes with hot pepper, soy sauce, chili powder, onion powder, a pinch of salt, black pepper and lime juice and whisk well.

2. Arrange beef medallions in a dish, pour sauce over them, toss and leave them aside for 2 hours.
3. Discard tomato marinade, put beef in your preheated Air Fryer and bake at 360°F for 10 minutes.
4. Divide steaks among plates and serve with a side salad. Enjoy!

Nutrition: calories 230, fat 4, fiber 1, carbs 13, protein 14

147. Chinese Steak and Broccoli

Preparation time: 45 minutes **Cooking time:** 12 minutes **Servings:** 4

Ingredients:

- ¾ pound round steak, cut into strips
- 1 pound broccoli florets
- 1/3 cup oyster sauce
- 2 teaspoons sesame oil
- 1 teaspoon soy sauce
- 1 teaspoon sugar
- 1/3 cup sherry
- 1 tablespoon olive oil
- 1 garlic clove, minced

Directions:

1. Mix sesame oil with oyster sauce, soy sauce, sherry and sugar, stir well and add beef.
2. Toss and leave aside for 30 minutes.
3. Transfer beef to a pan that fits your Air Fryer; add broccoli, garlic and oil, toss everything and cook at 380 degrees F for 12 minutes.
4. Divide among plates and serve. Enjoy!

Nutrition: calories 330, fat 12, fiber 7, crbs 23, protein 23

148. Coffee Flavored Steaks

Preparation time: 13 minutes **Cooking time:** 15 minutes **Servings**: 4

Ingredients:

- 1 and ½ tablespoons coffee, ground
- 4 rib-eye steaks
- ½ tablespoon sweet paprika
- 2 tablespoons chili powder
- 2 teaspoons garlic powder
- 2 teaspoons onion powder
- ¼ teaspoon ginger, ground
- ¼ teaspoon coriander, ground
- A pinch of cayenne pepper
- Black pepper to the taste

Directions:

1. Mix coffee with paprika, chili powder, garlic powder, onion powder, ginger, coriander, cayenne and black pepper, stir, rub steaks with this mix, put in preheated Air Fryer and bake at 360°F for 15 minutes.
2. Divide steaks among plates and serve with a side salad. Enjoy!

Nutrition: calories 160, fat 10, fiber 8, carbs 14, protein 12

149. Creamy Ham and Cauliflower

Preparation time: 15 minutes **Cooking time:** 4 hours

Servings: 6

Ingredients:

- 8 ounces of cheddar cheese, grated
- 4 cups ham, cubed
- 14 ounces of chicken stock
- ½ teaspoon garlic powder
- ½ teaspoon onion powder
- Salt and black pepper to the taste
- 4 garlic cloves, minced
- ¼ cup heavy cream

- 16 ounces cauliflower florets

Directions:

1. Mix ham with broth, cheese, cauliflower, salt, pepper, garlic powder, onion powder, garlic and heavy cream in a saucepan that fits your air fryer.
2. Put in your Air Fryer and bake at 300°F for 1 hour.
3. Divide into bowls and serve. Enjoy!

Nutrition: calories 322, fat 20, fiber 3, carbs 16, protein 23

150. Creamy Lamb

Preparation   time: 1-day **Cooking time:**1-hour **Servings**: 8

Ingredients:

- 5 pounds leg of lamb
- 2 cups of low-fat buttermilk
- 2 tablespoons of mustard
- ½ cup butter
- 2 tablespoons basil, minced
- 2 tablespoons tomato paste
- 2 garlic cloves, minced
- Salt and black pepper
- 1 cup of white wine
- 1 tbsp of cornstarch mixed with 1 tbsp of water
- ½ cup sour cream

Directions:

1. Place the lamb roast in a large dish, add the buttermilk, toss to coat, cover and refrigerate for 24 hours. Pat dry lamb in a pan that fits your Air Fryer.
2. Blend the butter with the tomato paste, mustard, basil, rosemary, salt, pepper and garlic. Spread over lamb, place everything in your fryer and bake at 300°F for 1 hour. Slice the lamb, divide among the plates, leave aside for the time being and heat the pan's cooking juices on the stovetop.

3. Add the wine, cornstarch, salt, pepper and sour cream, stir, remove from the heat, pour over the lamb and serve.
4. Enjoy!

Nutrition: calories 288, fat 4, fiber 7, carbs 19, protein 25

151. Garlic and Bell Pepper Beef

Preparation time: 33 minutes **Cooking time:** 30 minutes **Servings:** 4

Ingredients:

- 11 ounces steak fillets, sliced
- 4 garlic cloves, minced
- 2 tablespoons olive oil
- 1 red bell pepper, cut into strips
- Black pepper to the taste
- 1 tablespoon sugar
- 2 tablespoons fish sauce
- 2 teaspoons corn flour
- ½ cup beef stock
- 4 green onions, sliced

Directions:

1. Mix the beef with the oil, garlic, black pepper and bell pepper in a pan fitting your air fryer, stir, cover and store in the refrigerator for 30 minutes.
2. Place the skillet in your preheated air fryer and bake at 360°F for 14 minutes. Combine the sugar with the fish sauce in a bowl, mix well, pour over the beef and cook at 360°F for 7 minutes.
3. Add the broth to the corn flour and green onions, stir and cook at 370°F for an additional 7 minutes. Divide everything on plates and serve.

4. Enjoy!

Nutrition: cal. 344, fat 3, fiber 12, carbs 26, protein 38

152. Garlic Lamb Chops

Preparation time: 12 minutes **Cooking time:** 10 minutes **Servings:** 4

Ingredients:

- 3 tablespoons olive oil
- 8 lamb chops
- Salt and black pepper to the taste
- 4 garlic cloves, minced
- 1 tablespoon oregano, chopped
- 1 tablespoon coriander, chopped

Directions:

1. Blend the oregano with the salt, pepper, oil, garlic and lamb chops. Transfer the lamb chops to your
2. Air Fryer and bake it for 10 minutes at 400°F.
3. Spoon the lamb chops onto the plates and serve with a salad. Enjoy!

Nutrition: calories 230, fat 7, fiber 5, carbs 14, protein 23

153. Greek Beef Meatballs Salad

Preparation time: 14 minutes **Cooking time:** 10 minutes **Servings:** 6

Ingredients:

- ¼ cup milk
- 17 ounces beef, ground
- 1 yellow onion, grated
- 5 bread slices, cubed
- 1 egg, whisked
- ¼ cup parsley, chopped
- Salt and black pepper to the taste
- 2 garlic cloves, minced
- ¼ cup mint, chopped
- 2 and ½ teaspoons oregano, dried
- 1 tablespoon olive oil
- Cooking spray
- 7 ounces cherry tomatoes, halved
- 1 cup baby spinach

- 1 and ½ tablespoons of lemon juice
- 7 ounces Greek yogurt

Directions:

1. Put the toast in a bowl, add the milk, soak for a few minutes, press and transfer to another bowl. Add the beef, egg, salt, pepper, mint, parsley, oregano, garlic and onion.
2. Coat with cooking spray, place in your air fryer and bake at 370°F for 10 minutes. In a bowl, toss the spinach with the cucumber and tomato.
3. Add the meatballs, oil, salt, pepper, lemon juice and yogurt, mix and serve. Enjoy!

Nutrition: calories 201, fat 4, fiber 8, carbs 13, protein 27

154. Ham and Veggie Air Fried Mix

Preparation time: 13 minutes **Cooking time:** 20 minutes **Servings:** 6

Ingredients:

- ¼ cup butter
- ¼ cup flour
- 3 cups milk
- ½ teaspoon thyme, dried
- 2 cups ham, chopped
- 6 ounces sweet peas
- 4 ounces mushrooms, halved
- 1 cup baby carrots

Directions:

1. Heat a large pan that fits your Air Fryer with the butter over medium heat, melt it, add flour and whisk well.

2. Add milk and, well, again and take off the heat.
3. Add thyme, ham, peas, mushrooms and baby carrots, toss, put in your Air Fryer and bake at 360°F for 20 minutes.
4. Divide everything on plates and serve. Enjoy!

Nutrition: calories 311, fat 6, fiber 8, carbs 12, protein 7

155. Indian Pork

Preparation time: 37 minutes **Cooking time:** 10 minutes **Servings:** 4

Ingredients:

- 1 teaspoon ginger powder
- 2 teaspoons chili paste
- 2 garlic cloves, minced
- 14 ounces of pork chops, cubed
- 1 shallot, chopped
- 1 teaspoon coriander, ground
- 7 ounces of coconut milk
- 2 tablespoons olive oil
- 3 ounces peanuts, ground
- 3 tablespoons soy sauce
- Salt and black pepper

Directions:

1. Mix the ginger with 1 teaspoon of chili paste, half of the soy sauce, half of the garlic and half of the oil. Beat, add the meat, stir and let stand for 10 minutes.
2. Transfer the meat to your frying pan and cook at 400°F for 12 minutes, turning halfway. In the meantime, heat one pan with the remaining oil over medium-high heat.
3. Add the shallot, garlic, coriander, coconut milk, peanuts, chili paste and soy sauce. Toss and bake for 5 minutes.
4. Divide the pork among plates, place the coconut mixture among top and serve. Enjoy!

Nutrition: cal 424, fat 11, fiber 4, carbs 42, prote 18

156. Mexican Beef Mix

Preparation time: 16 minutes **Cooking time:** 1-hour and 10 minutes **Servings:** 8

Ingredients:

- 2 yellow onions, minced
- 2 tablespoons of olive oil
- 2 pounds beef roast, cubed
- 2 green bell peppers, chopped
- 1 habanero pepper, chopped
- 4 jalapenos, chopped
- 14 ounces canned tomatoes, chopped
- 2 tablespoons cilantro, chopped
- 6 garlic cloves, minced
- ½ cup water
- Salt and black pepper to the taste
- 1 and ½ teaspoons cumin, ground
- ½ cup black olives, pitted and chopped
- 1 teaspoon oregano, dried

Directions:

1. In a frying pan, mix the beef with the oil, green peppers, cilantro, oregano, onions, jalapenos, habanero pepper, tomatoes, garlic, water, cumin, salt and pepper.
2. Place your air fryer and bake at 300°F for 1 hour and 10 minutes.
3. Add the olives, toss, divide between bowls and serve. Enjoy!

Nutrition: calories 304, fat 14, fiber 4, carbs 18, protein. 25

157. Mustard Marinated Beef

Preparation time: 10 minutes **Cooking time:** 45 minutes **Servings:** 6

Ingredients:

- 6 bacon strips
- 2 tablespoons butter
- 3 garlic cloves, minced
- Salt and black pepper to the taste
- 1 tablespoon horseradish
- 1 tablespoon mustard
- 3 pounds of beef roast
- 1 and ¾ cup beef stock
- ¾ cup red wine

Directions:

1. Toss butter with mustard, garlic, salt, pepper and horseradish. Whisk and rub the beef with this mixture. Lay the bacon strips on a cutting board, place the beef on top, and add the bacon around the beef.
2. Transfer to your Air Fryer's basket, bake at 400°F for 15 minutes and transfer to a pan fitting your fryer. Add the stock and wine to the beef, put the pan in your fryer and cook at 360°F for 30 minutes more.
3. Cut the beef into pieces and serve with a side salad. Enjoy!

Nutrition: calories 500, fat 9, fiber 4, carbs 29, protein 36

158. Oriental Air Fried Lamb

Preparation time: 16 minutes **Cooking time:** 42 minutes. **Servings:** 8

Ingredients:

- 2 and ½ pounds of lamb shoulder, chopped
- 3 tablespoons honey
- 3 ounces almonds, peeled and chopped
- 9 ounces plumps, pitted
- 8 ounces of veggie stock
- 2 yellow onions, chopped
- 2 garlic cloves, minced
- Salt and black pepper to the tastes
- 1 teaspoon cumin powder
- 1 teaspoon turmeric powder
- 1 teaspoon ginger powder
- 1 teaspoon cinnamon powder
- 3 tablespoons olive oil

Directions:

1. Mix cinnamon powder with ginger, cumin,

turmeric, garlic, olive oil and lamb, toss to coat, place in your preheated Air Fryer and cook at 350°F for 8 minutes.

2. Transfer meat to a dish that fits your Air Fryer; add onions, stock, honey and plums, stir, introduce in your Air Fryer and cook at 350°F for 35 minutes.

3. Divide everything among plates and serve with almonds sprinkled on top. Enjoy!

Nutrition: cal. 432, fat 23, fiber 6, carbs 30, protein 20

159. Pork Chops and Green Beans

Preparation time: 17 minutes **Cooking time:** 15 minutes **Servings:** 4

Ingredients:

- 4 pork chops, bone-in
- 2 tablespoons olive oil
- 1 tablespoon sage, chopped
- Salt and black pepper to the taste
- 16 ounces green beans
- 3 garlic cloves, minced
- 2 tablespoons parsley, chopped

Directions:

1. Mix pork chops in a pan that fits your Air Fryer with olive oil, sage, salt, pepper, green beans, garlic and parsley, toss, introduce in your Air Fryer and bake at 360°F for 15 minutes.

2. Divide everything among plates. Enjoy!

Nutrition: calories 261, fat 7, fiber 9, carbs 14, protein 20

160. Pork Chops and Mushrooms

Preparation time: 16 minutes **Cooking time:** 40 minutes **Servings:** 3

Ingredients:

- 8 ounces mushrooms, sliced
- 1 teaspoon garlic powder
- 1 yellow onion, chopped
- 1 cup mayonnaise
- 3 pork chops, boneless
- 1 teaspoon nutmeg
- 1 tablespoon balsamic vinegar
- ½ cup olive oil

Directions:

1. Heat a pan that fits your Air Fryer with the oil over medium heat, add mushrooms and onions, stir and cook for 4 minutes.

2. Add pork chops, nutmeg and garlic powder and brown on both sides.

3. Introduce pan your Air Fryer at 330 degrees F and cook for 30 minutes.

4. Add vinegar and mayo, stir, divide everything among plates and serve. Enjoy!

Nutrition: calories 600, fat 10, fiber 1, carbs 8, protein 30

VEGETABLES

161. Beets and Blue Cheese Salad

Preparation time: 12 minutes **Cooking time:** 14 minutes **Servings:** 6

Ingredients:

- 6 beets, peeled and quartered
- Salt and black pepper to the taste
- ¼ cup blue cheese, crumbled
- 1 tablespoon olive oil

Directions:

1. Put beets in your Air Fryer, cook them at 350 degrees F for 14 minutes and transfer them to a bowl.
2. Add blue cheese, salt, pepper and oil, toss and serve. Enjoy!

Nutrition: calories 100, fat 4, fiber 4, carbs 10, protein 5

162. Beet Salad and Parsley Dressing

Preparation time: 13 minutes **Cooking time:** 14 minutes **Servings:** 4

Ingredients:

- 4 beets
- 2 tablespoons balsamic vinegar
- A bunch of parsley, chopped
- Salt and black pepper to the taste
- 1 tablespoon extra-virgin olive oil

- 1 garlic clove, chopped
- 2 tablespoons capers

Directions:

1. Place the beets into your Air Fryer and bake at 360°F for 14 minutes. Meanwhile, mix parsley with garlic, salt, pepper, olive oil and capers in a bowl and stir well.
2. Transfer the beets to a cutting board, allow them to cool down, peel them, cut them in a salad bowl.
3. Add the vinegar, add the parsley dressing on top and serve. Enjoy!

Nutrition: calories 70, fat 2, fiber 1, carbs 6, protein 4

163. Beet, Tomato and Goat Cheese

Preparation time: 30 minutes **Cooking time:** 14 minutes **Servings:** 8

Ingredients:

- 8 small beets, trimmed, peeled and halved
- 1 red onion, sliced
- 4 ounces goat cheese, crumbled
- 1 tablespoon balsamic vinegar
- Salt and black pepper to the taste
- 2 tablespoons sugar
- 1-pint mixed cherry tomatoes, halved
- 2 ounces pecans
- 2 tablespoons olive oil

Directions:

1. Place the beets in your fryer, season them with salt and pepper, cook at 350 degrees F for 14 minutes and transfer to a bowl.
2. Add the onion, cherry tomatoes and pecans and blend. Toss the vinegar with the sugar and oil in another bowl. Whisk until the sugar dissolves and add to the salad.

3. Stir in the goat cheese, then serve. Enjoy!

Nutrition: calories 124, fat 7, fiber 5, carbs 12, protein 6

164. Cheesy Artichokes

Preparation time: 14 minutes Cooking time: 6 minutes Servings: 6

Ingredients:

- 14 ounces canned artichoke hearts
- 8 ounces of cream cheese
- 16 ounces parmesan cheese, grated
- 10 ounces spinach
- ½ cup chicken stock
- 8 ounces mozzarella, shredded
- ½ cup sour cream
- 3 garlic cloves, minced
- ½ cup mayonnaise
- 1 teaspoon onion powder

Directions:

1. Mix artichokes with stock, garlic, spinach, cream cheese, sour cream, onion powder and mayo in a pan that fits your Air Fryer.
2. Toss, introduce in your Air Fryer and bake at 350°F for 6 minutes.
3. Add mozzarella and Parmesan, serve. Enjoy!

Nutrition: cal. 261, fat 12, fiber 2, carbs 12, protei 15

165. Cheesy Brussels Sprouts

Preparation time: 14 minutes Cooking time: 8 minutes Servings: 4

Ingredients:

- 1 pound Brussels sprouts, washed
- Juice of 1 lemon
- Salt and black pepper to the taste
- 2 tablespoons butter
- 3 tablespoons parmesan, grated

Directions:

1. Put Brussels sprouts in your Air Fryer, cook

them at 350°F for 8 minutes and transfer to a bowl.

2. Heat a pan with the butter over medium heat; add lemon juice, salt and pepper, whisk well and add to Brussels sprouts. Add parmesan, toss until parmesan melts and serve. Enjoy!

Nutrition: calories 152, fat 6, fiber 6, carbs 8, prot 12

166. Cherry Tomatoes Skewers

Preparation time: 35 minutes Cooking time: 6 minutes Servings: 4

Ingredients:

- 3 tablespoons balsamic vinegar
- 24 cherry tomatoes
- 2 tablespoons olive oil
- 3 garlic cloves, minced
- 1 tablespoons thyme, chopped
- Salt and black pepper to the taste

For the dressing:

- 2 tablespoons balsamic vinegar
- Salt and black pepper to the taste
- 4 tablespoons olive oil

Directions:

1. Combine 2 tablespoons of oil with 3 tablespoons of vinegar, 3 cloves of garlic, thyme, salt and black pepper and beat well.
2. Add the tomatoes, stir to coat and let rest for 30 minutes. Place 6 tomatoes on a skewer, then repeat with the rest. Add them to your fryer and cook at 360F for 6 minutes.
3. Combine 2 tablespoons of vinegar with the salt, pepper and 4 tablespoons of oil in another bowl and beat well.
4. Place the tomato brochettes on the plates and serve with the dressing sprinkled on top. Enjoy!

Nutrition: calories 142, fat 1, fiber 1, carbs 2, protein 7

167. Collard Greens and Bacon

Preparation time: 12 minutes Cooking time: 12 minutes Servings: 4

Ingredients:

- 1 pound collard greens
- 3 bacon strips, chopped
- ¼ cup cherry tomatoes halved
- 1 tablespoon apple cider vinegar
- 2 tablespoons chicken stock
- Salt and black pepper to the taste

Directions:

1. Heat a pan that fits your Air Fryer over medium heat, add bacon, stir and cook for 1-2 minutes.
2. Add tomatoes, collard greens, vinegar, stock, salt and pepper, stir, introduce in your Air Fryer and cook at 320 degrees F for 10 minutes.
3. Divide among plates and serve. Enjoy!

Nutrition: calories 120, fat 3, fiber 1, carbs 3, prot 7

168. Collard Greens and Turkey Wings

Preparation time: 14 minutes **Cooking time:** 20 minutes **Servings**: 6

Ingredients:

- 1 sweet onion, chopped
- 2 smoked turkey wings
- 2 tablespoons olive oil
- 3 garlic cloves, minced
- 2 and ½ pounds of collard greens, chopped
- Salt and black pepper to the taste
- 2 tablespoons apple cider vinegar
- 1 tablespoon brown sugar
- ½ teaspoon crushed red pepper

Directions:

1. Heat a pan that fits your Air Fryer with the oil over medium-high heat, add onions, stir and cook for 2 minutes.
2. Add garlic, greens, vinegar, salt, pepper, crushed red pepper, sugar and smoked turkey
3. Introduce in preheated Air Fryer and cook at 350°F for 15 minutes.
4. Divide greens and turkey among plates and serve.
5. Enjoy!

Nutrition: calories 262, fat 4, fiber 8, carbs 12, protein 4

169. Collard Greens

Preparation time: 16 minutes **Cooking time:** 10 minutes **Servings:** 4

Ingredients:

- 1 bunch of collard greens, trimmed
- 2 tablespoons olive oil
- 2 tablespoons tomato puree
- 1 yellow onion, chopped
- 3 garlic cloves, minced
- Salt and black pepper to the taste
- 1 tablespoon balsamic vinegar
- 1 teaspoon sugar

Directions:

1. Mix oil, garlic, vinegar, onion and tomato puree and whisk in a dish that fits your Air Fryer.
2. Add collard greens, salt, pepper and sugar, toss, introduce in your Air Fryer and cook at 320 degrees F for 10 minutes.
3. Divide collard greens, mix on plates.
4. Enjoy!

Nutrition: calories 121, fat 3, fiber 3, carbs 7, prot 3

170. Creamy Green Beans

Preparation time: 11 minutes **Cooking time:** 15 minutes **Servings:** 4

Ingredients:

- ½ cup heavy cream
- 1 cup mozzarella, shredded

- 2/3 cup parmesan, grated
- Salt and black pepper to the taste
- 2 pounds of green beans
- 2 teaspoons lemon zest, grated
- A pinch of red pepper flakes

Directions:

1. Put the beans in a dish that fits your Air Fryer, add heavy cream, salt, pepper, lemon zest, pepper flakes, mozzarella and parmesan, toss, introduce in your Air Fryer and cook at 350°F for 15 minutes.
2. Divide among plates and serve.
3. Enjoy!

Nutrition: calories 231, fat 6, fiber 7, carbs 8, protein 5

171. Crispy Potatoes and Parsley

Preparation time: 8 minutes **Cooking time:** 10 minutes **Servings:** 4

Ingredients:

- 1 pound gold potatoes, cut into wedges
- Salt and black pepper to the taste
- 2 tablespoons olive
- Juice from ½ lemon
- ¼ cup parsley leaves, chopped

Directions:

1. Rub potatoes with salt, pepper, lemon juice and olive oil, put them in your Air Fryer and cook at 350 degrees F for 10 minutes.
2. Divide among plates, sprinkle parsley on top and serve.
3. Enjoy!

Nutrition: calories 152, fat 3, fiber 7, carbs 17, protein 4

172. Easy Green Beans and Potatoes

Preparation time: 13 minutes **Cooking time:** 15 minutes **Servings:** 5

Ingredients:

- 2 pounds of green beans
- 6 new potatoes, halved
- Salt and black pepper to the taste
- A drizzle of olive oil
- 6 bacon slices, cooked and chopped

Directions:

1. In a bowl, mix green beans with potatoes, salt, pepper and oil, toss, transfer to your Air Fryer and cook at 390 degrees F for 15 minutes.
2. Divide
3. among plates and serve with bacon sprinkled on top. Enjoy!

Nutrition: cal. 374, fat 15, fiber 12, carbs 28, prot 12

173. Indian Potatoes

Preparation time: 12 minutes **Cooking time:** 12 minutes **Servings:** 4

Ingredients:

- 1 tablespoon coriander seeds
- 1 tablespoon cumin seeds
- Salt and black pepper to the taste
- ½ teaspoon turmeric powder
- ½ teaspoon red chili powder
- 1 teaspoon pomegranate powder
- 1 tablespoon pickled mango, chopped
- 2 teaspoons fenugreek, dried

- 5 potatoes, boiled, peeled and cubed
- 2 tablespoons olive oil

Directions:

1. Heat a pan that fits your Air Fryer with the oil over medium heat, add coriander and cumin seeds, stir and cook for 2 minutes.
2. Add salt, pepper, turmeric, chili powder, pomegranate powder, mango, fenugreek and potatoes, toss, introduce in your Air Fryer and bake at 360°F for 10 minutes.
3. Divide among plates and serve hot. Enjoy!

Nutrition: calories 251, fat 7, fiber 4, carbs 12, protein 7

174. Indian Turnips Salad

Preparation time: 11 minutes **Cooking time:** 12 minutes **Servings:** 4

Ingredients:

- 20 ounces of turnips, peeled and chopped
- 1 teaspoon garlic, minced
- 1 teaspoon ginger, grated
- 2 yellow onions, chopped
- 2 tomatoes, chopped
- 1 teaspoon cumin, ground
- 1 teaspoon coriander, ground
- 2 green chilies, chopped
- ½ teaspoon turmeric powder
- 2 tablespoons butter
- Salt and black pepper to the taste
- A handful of coriander leaves, chopped

Directions:

1. Heat a pan that fits your Air Fryer with the butter, melt it, add green chilies, garlic and ginger, stir and cook for 1 minute.
2. Add onions, salt, pepper, tomatoes, turmeric, cumin, ground coriander and turnips, stir, introduce in your Air Fryer and bake at 350°F for 10 minutes.
3. Divide among plates, sprinkle fresh

coriander on top and serve. Enjoy!

Nutrition: calories 100, fat 3, fiber 6, carbs 12, protein 4

175. Italian Eggplant Stew

Preparation time: 13 minutes **Cooking time:** 15 minutes **Servings:** 4

Ingredients:

- 1 red onion, chopped
- 2 garlic cloves, chopped
- 1 bunch of parsley, chopped
- Salt and black pepper to the taste
- 1 teaspoon oregano, dried
- 2 eggplants, cut into medium chunks
- 2 tablespoons olive oil
- 2 tablespoons capers, chopped
- 1 handful of green olives, pitted and sliced
- 5 tomatoes, chopped
- 3 tablespoons herb vinegar

Directions:

1. Heat a pan that fits your Air Fryer with the oil over medium heat, add eggplant, oregano, salt and pepper, stir and bake for 5 minutes.
2. Add garlic, onion, parsley, capers, olives, vinegar and tomatoes, stir, introduce in your Air Fryer and cook at 360 degrees F for 15 minutes. Divide into bowls and serve. Enjoy!

Nutrition: calories 170, fat 13, fiber 3, carbs 5, protein 7

176. Mexican Peppers

Preparation time: 9 minutes **Cooking time:** 25 minutes **Servings:** 4

Ingredients:

- 4 bell peppers, sliced leaves and seeds removed
- ½ cup tomato juice
- 2 tablespoons jarred jalapenos, chopped
- 4 chicken breasts

- 1 cup tomatoes, chopped
- ¼ cup yellow onion, chopped
- ¼ cup green peppers, chopped
- 2 cups tomato sauce
- Salt and black pepper to the taste
- 2 teaspoons onion powder
- ½ teaspoon red pepper, crushed
- 1 teaspoon chili powder
- ½ teaspoons garlic powder
- 1 teaspoon cumin, ground

Directions:

1. In a pan that fits your Air Fryer, mix chicken breasts with tomato juice, jalapenos, tomatoes, onion, green peppers, salt, pepper, onion powder, red pepper, chili powder, garlic powder, oregano and cumin, stir well, introduce in your Air Fryer and cook at 350 degrees F for 15 minutes,
2. Shred meat using 2 forks, stir, stuff bell peppers with this mix, place them in your Air Fryer and cook at 320°F for 10 minutes more.
3. Divide stuffed peppers on plates. Enjoy!

Nutrition: calo 180, fat 4, fiber 3, carbs 7, protein 14

177. Sesame Mustard Greens

Preparation time: 10 minutes **Cooking time:** 11 minutes **Servings:** 4

Ingredients:

- 2 garlic cloves, minced
- 1 pound mustard greens, torn
- 1 tablespoon olive oil
- ½ cup yellow onion, sliced
- Salt and black pepper to the taste

- 3 tablespoons veggie stock
- ¼ teaspoon dark sesame oil

Directions:

1. Heat a pan that fits your Air Fryer with the oil over medium heat, add onions, stir and brown them for 5 minutes.
2. Add garlic, stock, greens, salt and pepper, stir, introduce in your Air Fryer and cook at 350°F for 6 minutes.
3. Add sesame oil, toss to coat, divide among plates and serve. Enjoy!

Nutrition: calories 120, fat 3, fiber 1, carbs 3, prot 7

178. Simple Stuffed Tomatoes

Preparation time: 10 minutes **Cooking time:** 15 minutes **Servings:** 4

Ingredients:

- 4 tomatoes, tops cut off and pulp scooped and chopped
- Salt and black pepper to the taste
- 1 yellow onion, chopped
- 1 tablespoon butter
- 2 tablespoons celery, chopped
- ½ cup mushrooms, chopped
- 1 tablespoon breadcrumbs
- 1 cup cottage cheese
- ¼ teaspoon caraway seeds
- 1 tablespoon parsley, chopped

Directions:

1. Heat a pan with the butter over medium heat, melt it, add onion and celery, stir and cook for 3 minutes.
2. Add tomato pulp and mushrooms, stir and cook for 1 minute more.
3. Add salt, pepper, crumbled bread, cheese, caraway seeds and parsley, stir, cook for 4 minutes more and take off the heat.
4. Stuff tomatoes with this mix, place them in your Air Fryer and cook at 350°F for 8 minutes.

5. Divide stuffed tomatoes on plates. Enjoy!

Nutrition: calories 143, fat 4, fiber 6, carbs 4, prot 4

179. Simple Tomatoes and Bell Pepper Sauce

Preparation time: 14 minutes **Cooking time:** 15 minutes **Servings:** 4

Ingredients:

- 2 red bell peppers, chopped
- 2 garlic cloves, minced
- 1 pound cherry tomatoes, halved
- 1 teaspoon rosemary, dried
- 3 bay leaves
- 2 tablespoons olive oil
- 1 tablespoon balsamic vinegar
- Salt and black pepper to the taste

Directions:

1. In a bowl, mix tomatoes with garlic, salt, black pepper, rosemary, bay leaves, half of the oil and half of the vinegar, toss to coat, introduce in your Air Fryer and roast them at 320°F for 15 minutes.
2. Meanwhile, mix bell peppers with a pinch of sea salt, black pepper, the oil and the vinegar in your food processor and blend very well.
3. Divide roasted tomatoes among plates, drizzle the bell peppers sauce over them and serve. Enjoy!

Nutrition: calories 123, fat 1, fiber 1, carbs 8, protein 10

180. Spanish Greens

Preparation time: 14 minutes **Cooking time:** 8 minutes **Servings:** 4

Ingredients:

- 1 apple, cored and chopped
- 1 yellow onion, sliced
- 3 tablespoons olive oil
- ¼ cup raisins
- 6 garlic cloves, chopped
- ¼ cup pine nuts, toasted
- ¼ cup balsamic vinegar
- 5 cups mixed spinach and chard
- Salt and black pepper to the taste
- A pinch of nutmeg

Directions:

1. Heat a pan that fits your Air Fryer with the oil over medium-high heat, add onion, stir and cook for 3 minutes.
2. Add apple, garlic, raisins, vinegar, mixed spinach and chard, nutmeg, salt and pepper, stir, introduce in preheated Air Fryer and cook at 350 degrees F for 5 minutes. Divide among plates, sprinkle pine nuts on top and serve. Enjoy!

Nutrition: calories 120, fat 1, fiber 2, carbs 3, protein 6

DESSERTS

181. Blueberry Scones

Preparation time: 11 minutes **Cooking time:** 10 minutes **Servings:** 10

Ingredients:

- 1 cup white flour
- 1 cup blueberries
- 2 eggs
- ½ cup heavy cream
- ½ cup butter
- 5 tablespoons sugar
- 2 teaspoons vanilla extract
- 2 teaspoons baking powder

Directions:

1. Mix the flour, salt, baking powder and blueberries into a bowl.
2. Mix heavy cream with butter, vanilla extract, sugar and eggs in another bowl, and stir well.
3. Combine the 2 mixtures, knead until you obtain your dough, shape 10 triangles from this mix, put them on a lined baking sheet suitable to your Air Fryer and cook them at 320°F for 10 minutes. Serve them cold. Enjoy!

Nutrition: calories 130, fat 2, fiber 2, carbs 4, protein 3

182. Bread Dough and Amaretto Dessert

Preparation time: 13 minutes **Cooking time:** 12 minutes **Servings:** 12

Ingredients:

- 1 pound bread dough
- 1 cup sugar
- ½ cup butter, melted
- 1 cup heavy cream
- 12 ounces chocolate chips
- 2 tablespoons amaretto liqueur

Directions:

1. Roll the dough, cut it into 20 slices and then cut each one slice in halves.
2. Brush dough pieces with butter, sprinkle sugar, place them in your Air Fryer's basket after you've brushed it some butter, cook them at 350 degrees F for 5 minutes, flip them, cook for 3 minutes more and transfer to a platter.
3. Heat a pan with the heavy cream over medium heat, add chocolate chips and stir until they melt.
4. Add liqueur, stir again, transfer to a bowl and serve bread dippers with this sauce. Enjoy!

Nutrition: calories 200, fat 1, fiber 0, carbs 6, prot 6

183. Bread Pudding

Preparation time: 10 minutes **Cooking time:** 1-hour **Servings:** 4

Ingredients:

- 6 glazed doughnuts, crumbled
- 1 cup cherries
- 4 egg yolks
- 1 and ½ cups whipping cream
- ½ cup raisins

- ¼ cup sugar
- ½ cup chocolate chips.

Directions:

1. Mix cherries with egg yolks and whipping cream and stir well. Mix raisins with sugar, chocolate chips and doughnuts in another bowl and stir.
2. Combine the 2 mixtures, transfer everything to a greased pan suitable to your Air Fryer and cook at 310°F for 1 hour.
3. Chill the pudding before cutting. Enjoy!

Nutrition: calories 302, fat 8, fiber 2, carbs 23, protein 10

184. Cocoa Cookies

Preparation time: 13 minutes **Cooking time:** 14 minutes **Servings:** 12

Ingredients:

- 6 ounces of coconut oil, melted
- 6 eggs
- 3 ounces cocoa powder
- 2 teaspoons vanilla
- ½ teaspoon baking powder
- 4 ounces of cream cheese
- 5 tablespoons sugar

Directions:

1. Mix eggs with coconut oil, cocoa powder, baking powder, vanilla, and cream cheese in a blender and swerve and stir using a mixer.
2. Pour this into a lined baking dish suitable your Air Fryer, introduce in the fryer at 320 degrees F and bake for 14 minutes.
3. Slice the cookie sheet into rectangles. Enjoy!

Nutrition: calories 178, fat 14, fiber 2, carbs 3, protein 5

185. Coffee Cheesecakes

Preparation time: 10 minutes **Cooking time:** 20 minutes **Servings:** 6

Ingredients:

For the cheesecakes:

- 2 tablespoons butter
- 8 ounces of cream cheese
- 3 tablespoons coffee
- 3 eggs
- 1/3 cup sugar
- 1 tablespoon caramel syrup

For the frosting:

- 3 tablespoons caramel syrup
- 3 tablespoons butter
- 8 ounces mascarpone cheese, soft
- 2 tablespoons sugar

Directions:

1. In your blender, mix cream cheese with eggs, 2 tablespoons butter, coffee, 1 tablespoon caramel syrup and 1/3 cup sugar and pulse very well.
2. Spoon into cupcakes pan suitable to your Air Fryer, introduce in the fryer, cook at 320°F and bake for 20 minutes. Leave aside to cool down and keep in the freezer for 3 hours.
3. Meanwhile, in a bowl, mix 3 tablespoons butter with 3 tablespoons caramel syrup, 2 tablespoons sugar and mascarpone, blend well, spoon this over cheesecakes and serve them. Enjoy!

Nutrition: calories 254, fat 23, fiber 0, carbs 21, protein 5

186. Crispy Apples

Preparation time: 16 minutes **Cooking time:** 10 minutes **Servings:** 4

Ingredients:

- 2 teaspoons cinnamon powder
- 5 apples, cored and cut into chunks
- ½ teaspoon nutmeg powder
- 1 tablespoon maple syrup
- ½ cup water
- 4 tablespoons butter
- ¼ cup flour
- ¾ cup old-fashioned rolled oats
- ¼ cup brown sugar

Directions:

1. Put the apples in a pan suitable to your Air Fryer and add cinnamon, nutmeg, maple syrup and water.
2. In a bowl, mix butter with oats, sugar, salt and flour, stir, drop spoonful of this mix on top of apples, introduce in your Air Fryer and cook at 350°F for 10 minutes.
3. Serve warm. Enjoy!

Nutrition: calories 200, fat 6, fiber 8, carbs 29, protein 12

187. Lemon Tart

Preparation time: 1-hour **Cooking time:** 35 minutes **Servings:** 6

Ingredients:

For the crust:

- 2 tablespoons sugar
- 2 cups white flour
- A pinch of salt
- 3 tablespoons ice water
- 12 tablespoons cold butter

For the filling:

- 2 eggs, whisked

- 1 and ¼ cup sugar
- 10 tablespoons melted and chilled butter
- Juice from 2 lemons
- Zest from 2 lemons, grated

Directions:

1. Combine 2 cups of flour with salt and 2 tablespoons of sugar and beat. Add 12 tablespoons of butter and water, knead to make a paste, form a ball, wrap in aluminum foil and refrigerate for 1 hour.
2. Transfer the dough to a floured surface, flatten, place on the bottom of a pie pan, pierce with a fork and keep in the refrigerator for 20 minutes. Place in your fryer at 360°F and bake for 15 minutes.
3. Mix 1 and ¼ cups of sugar with the eggs, 10 tbsp. of butter, lemon juice and lemon zest and whisk well. Pour into the pie crust, spread evenly, introduce into the air fryer and cook at 360°F for 20 minutes. Cut and serve it.
4. Enjoy!

Nutrition: calories 183, fat 4, fiber 1, carbs 2, protein 3

188. Mandarin Pudding

Preparation time: 22 minutes **Cooking time:** 40 minutes **Servings:** 8

Ingredients:

- 1 mandarin, peeled and sliced
- Juice from 2 mandarins
- 2 tablespoons brown sugar
- 4 ounces butter, soft
- 2 eggs, whisked
- ¾ cup sugar
- ¾ cup white flour
- ¾ cup almonds, ground
- Honey for serving

Directions:

1. Grease a loaf pan with some butter, sprinkle the brown sugar on the base and arrange the

tangerine slices.

2. Blend the butter with the sugar, eggs, almonds, flour and tangerine juice. Place the skillet in your deep fryer and cook 360°F for 40 minutes.

3. Spoon the pudding onto a plate and serve with the honey. Enjoy!

Nutrition: calories 163, fat 3, fiber 2, carbs 3, protein 6

189. Maple Cupcakes

Preparation time: 13 minutes **Cooking time:** 20 minutes **Servings:** 4

Ingredients:

- 4 tablespoons butter
- 4 eggs
- ½ cup pure applesauce
- 2 teaspoons cinnamon powder
- 1 teaspoon vanilla extract
- ½ apple, cored and chopped
- 4 teaspoons maple syrup
- ¾ cup white flour
- ½ teaspoon baking powder

Directions:

1. Heat skillet with butter at medium heat; add applesauce, vanilla, eggs and maple syrup, toss, remove heat and allow to cool.

2. Add the flour, cinnamon, baking powder and apples, whisk, and pour into a cupcake mold. Transfer to the 350°F air fryer and bake for 20 minutes.

3. Cool the cupcakes, place them on a plate and serve.

4. Enjoy!

Nutrition: calories 152, fat 3, fiber 1, carbs 5, protein 4

190. Mini Lava Cakes

Preparation time: 14 minutes **Cooking time:** 20 minutes **Servings:** 3

Ingredients:

- 1 egg
- 4 tablespoons sugar
- 2 tablespoons olive oil
- 4 tablespoons milk
- 4 tablespoons flour
- 1 tablespoon cocoa powder
- ½ teaspoon baking powder
- ½ teaspoon orange zest

Directions:

1. Mix egg with sugar, oil, milk, flour, salt, cocoa powder, baking powder and orange zest, stir well and pour this into greased ramekins.

2. Add ramekins to your Air Fryer and cook at 320°F for 20 minutes.

3. Serve lava cakes warm. Enjoy!

Nutrition: calories 201, fat 7, fiber 8, carbs 23, protein 4

191. Passion Fruit Pudding

Preparation time: 12 minutes **Cooking time:** 40 minutes **Servings:** 6

Ingredients:

- 1 cup Paleo passion fruit curd
- 4 passion fruits, pulp and seeds
- 3 and ½ ounces of maple syrup
- 3 eggs
- 2 ounces ghee, melted

- 3 and ½ ounces almond milk
- ½ cup of almond flour
- ½ teaspoon baking powder

Directions:

1. Mix half the curdled fruit with the passion fruit's seeds and pulp. Stir and divide into 6 heat- resistant ramekins.
2. Beat the eggs with the maple syrup, ghee, remaining curd, baking powder, milk and flour and toss to combine.
3. Divide into the ramekins, place them in the air fryer and cook at 200°F for 40 minutes.
4. Let the puddings chill and serve! Enjoy!

Nutrition: calories 432, fat 22, fiber 3, carbs 7, protein 8

192. Peach Pie

Preparation time: 14 minutes **Cooking time:** 35 minutes **Servings**: 4

Ingredients:

- 1 pie dough
- 2 and ¼ pounds of peaches, pitted and chopped
- 2 tablespoons cornstarch
- ½ cup sugar
- 2 tablespoons flour
- A pinch of nutmeg, ground
- 1 tablespoon dark rum
- 1 tablespoon lemon juice
- 2 tablespoons butter, melted

Directions:

1. Roll the pastry in a mold that fits your air fryer and press well. Mix well with the peaches, cornstarch, flour, nutmeg, rum, sugar, lemon juice and butter.
2. Pour and spread this pie pan, place in your air fryer and cook at 350°F for 35 minutes.
3. Serve warm or cold. Enjoy!

Nutrition: calories 232, fat 6, fiber 7, carbs 9, prot 5

193. Pears and Espresso Cream

Preparation time: 13 minutes **Cooking time:** 30 minutes **Servings:** 4

Ingredients:

- 4 pears, halved and cored
- 2 tablespoons lemon juice
- 1 tablespoon sugar
- 2 tablespoons water
- 2 tablespoons butter

For the cream:

- 1 cup whipping cream
- 1 cup mascarpone
- 1/3 cup sugar
- 2 tablespoons espresso, cold

Directions:

1. Combine pear halves with lemon juice, 1 tablespoon sugar, butter and water, mix well, transfer to fryer and cook at 360°F for 30 minutes.
2. Meanwhile, in a bowl, combine the whipping cream with the mascarpone, 1/3 cup of sugar and the espresso. Whisk well, then refrigerate until the pears have cooked.
3. Arrange pears on plates, garnish with espresso cream and serve. Enjoy!

Nutrition: calories 212, fat 5, fiber 7, carbs 8, prot 7

194. Plum and Currant Tart

Preparation time: 34 minutes **Cooking time:** 35 minutes **Servings**: 6

Ingredients:

For the crumble:

- ¼ cup almond flour
- ¼ cup millet flour
- 1 cup brown rice flour
- ½ cup cane sugar
- 10 tablespoons butter, soft

- 3 tablespoons milk

For the filling:

- 1-pound small plums pitted and halved
- 1 cup white currants
- 2 tablespoons cornstarch
- 3 tablespoons sugar
- ½ teaspoon vanilla extract
- ½ teaspoon cinnamon powder
- ¼ teaspoon ginger powder
- 1 teaspoon lime juice

Directions:

1. Combine the brown rice flour with ½ cup sugar, butter and milk, millet flour, almond flour, and stir to obtain a sandy dough. Reserve ¼ of the dough, press the rest into a tart pan suitable to your air fryer and refrigerate for 30 minutes.
2. Meanwhile, in a bowl, combine the plums with the currants, 3 tablespoons of sugar, starch, vanilla extract, cinnamon, ginger and lime juice.
3. Pour over the pie crust, crumble the reserved dough on top, put in your fryer and bake at 350°F for 35 minutes.
4. Let it cool down, slice and serve. Enjoy!

Nutrition: calories 201, fat 5, fiber 4, carbs 8, prot 6

195. Plum Bars

Preparation time: 13 minutes **Cooking time:** 16 minutes **Servings:** 8

Ingredients:

- 2 cups dried plums
- 6 tablespoons water
- 2 cup rolled oats
- 1 cup brown sugar
- ½ teaspoon baking soda
- 1 teaspoon cinnamon powder
- 2 tablespoons butter, melted
- 1 egg, whisked
- Cooking spray

Directions:

1. Mix the plums with water in your food processor and stir to make a sticky paste. Combine the oats with the cinnamon, baking soda, sugar, egg and butter and beat well.
2. Press half of the oatmeal mixture into a baking dish that suits your fryer sprayed with cooking oil. Divide the plum mixture and garnish with the remaining half of the oatmeal mixture.
3. Put in the fryer and cook at 350°F for 16 minutes.
4. Set aside to cool down, cut into medium bars and serve. Enjoy!

Nutrition: calories 112, fat 5, fiber 6, carbs 12, protein 6

196. Plum Cake

Preparation time: 1 hour and 21 minutes
Cooking time: 35 minutes **Servings:** 8

Ingredients:

- 7 ounces flour
- 1 package of dried yeast
- 1-ounce butter, soft
- 1 egg, whisked
- 5 tablespoons sugar
- 3 ounces of warm milk
- 1 and ¾ pounds of plums, pitted and cut into quarters
- Zest from 1 lemon, grated
- 1-ounce almond flakes

Directions:

1. Mix the yeast with the butter, flour and 3 tablespoons of sugar. Add the milk and egg and whisk for 4 minutes until you get a paste.
2. Place the dough in a spring-loaded pan that fits the fryer you greased with butter, cover and set aside for 1 hour. Arrange plums on butter, sprinkle with remaining sugar.
3. Put in the fryer at 350 degrees F, cook for 36 minutes, cool, sprinkle with the almond flakes and lemon zest on top, slice and serve. Enjoy!

Nutrition: calories 193, fat 4, fiber 2, carbs 6, prot 7

197. Poppyseed Cake

Preparation time: 13 minutes **Cooking time:** 30 minutes **Servings:** 6

Ingredients:

- 1 and ¼ cups flour
- 1 teaspoon baking powder
- ¾ cup sugar
- 1 tablespoon orange zest, grated
- 2 teaspoons lime zest, grated
- ½ cup butter, soft
- 2 eggs, whisked
- ½ teaspoon vanilla extract
- 2 tablespoons poppy seeds
- 1 cup milk

For the cream:

- 1 cup sugar
- ½ cup passion fruit puree
- 3 tablespoons butter, melted
- 4 egg yolks

Directions:

1. Mix flour with baking powder, ¾ cup sugar, orange zest and lime zest and stir.
2. Add ½ cup butter, eggs, poppy seeds, vanilla and milk, stir using your mixer, pour into a cake pan that fits your Air

Fryer and cook at 350°F for about 30 minutes.
3. Meanwhile, heat a pan with 3 tablespoons butter at medium heat, add sugar and stir until it dissolves.
4. Take off the heat, add passion fruit puree and egg yolks gradually and whisk well.
5. Take the cake out of the fryer, cool it down and cut it into halves horizontally.
6. Spread ¼ of passion fruit cream over one half, top with the other cake half and spread ¼ of the cream. Serve cold.

Nutrition: calories 314, fat 16.4, fiber 0.8, carbs 40.1, protein 3.9

198. Pumpkin Cookies

Preparation time: 14 minutes **Cooking time:** 15 minutes **Servings:** 24

Ingredients:

- 2 and ½ cups flour
- ½ teaspoon baking soda
- 1 tablespoon flax seed, ground
- 3 tablespoons water
- ½ cup pumpkin flesh, mashed
- ¼ cup honey
- 2 tablespoons butter
- 1 teaspoon vanilla extract
- ½ cup dark chocolate chips

Directions:

1. Mix flax seed with water in a bowl, stir and leave aside for a few minutes.
2. In another bowl, mix flour with salt and baking soda.
3. Mix honey with pumpkin puree, butter, vanilla extract and flaxseed in a third bowl.
4. Combine flour with honey mix and chocolate chips and stir.
5. Scoop 1 tablespoon of cookie dough on a lined baking sheet that fits your Air Fryer, repeat with the rest of the dough, introduce

them in your Air Fryer and cook at 350 degrees F for 15 minutes.

6. Leave cookies to cool down and serve.Enjoy!

Nutrition: calories 140, fat 2, fiber 2, carbs 7, prot 10

199. Sweet Squares

Preparation time: 13 minutes **Cooking time:** 30 minutes **Servings:** 6

Ingredients:

- 1 cup flour
- ½ cup butter, soft
- 1 cup sugar
- ¼ cup powdered sugar
- 2 teaspoons lemon peel, grated
- 2 tablespoons lemon juice
- 2 eggs, whisked
- ½ teaspoon baking powder

Directions:

1. Mix flour with powdered sugar and butter in a bowl, stir well, press on the bottom of a pan that fits your air fryer, introduce in the fryer and bake at 350 degrees F for 14 minutes.
2. Mix sugar with lemon juice, lemon peel, eggs and baking powder in another bowl, stir using your mixer and spread over the baked crust.
3. Bake for 15 minutes more, leave aside to cool down, cut into medium squares and serve cold. Enjoy!

Nutrition: calories 100, fat 4, fiber 1, carbs 12, protein 1

200. Tangerine Cake

Preparation time: 11 minutes **Cooking time:** 20 minutes **Servings:** 8

Ingredients:

- ¾ cup sugar
- 2 cups flour
- ¼ cup olive oil
- ½ cup milk

- 1 teaspoon cider vinegar
- ½ teaspoon vanilla extract
- Juice and zest from 2 lemons
- Juice and zest from 1 tangerine
- Tangerine segments for serving

Directions:

1. In a bowl, mix flour with sugar and stir.
2. Mix oil with milk, vinegar, vanilla extract, lemon juice and zest in another bowl, and tangerine zest and whisk very well.
3. Add flour, stir well, pour this into a cake pan that fits your Air Fryer, introduce in the fryer and cook at 360 degrees F for 20 minutes.
4. Serve right away with tangerine segments on top. Enjoy!

Nutrition: calories 190, fat 1, fiber 1, carbs 4, protein 4

CONCLUSION

Air frying is one of the most popular cooking methods these days and Air Fryers have become one of the most amazing tools in the kitchen.

Air Fryers help you cook healthy and delicious meals in no time! You don't need to be an expert in the kitchen to cook special dishes for you and your loved ones!

You just must own an Air Fryer and this great Air Fryer cookbook!

You will soon make the best dishes ever and you will impress everyone around you with your home-cooked meals!

Just trust us! Get your hands on an air fryer and on this useful Air Fryer recipes collection and start your new cooking experience! Have fun!

Printed in Great Britain
by Amazon